RUN THE NUMBERS

DON'T LET THE NUMBERS RUN OVER YOU!

**Improve Your Chances of Making the
Right Decision by Understanding and
Utilizing the Tools and Techniques
of
MANAGERIAL ACCOUNTING**

By

Donald R. Dignam MBA, CPA

Adjunct Lecturer In Accounting
Indiana University South Bend

ISBN: 1-4107-0736-9 (E-book)
ISBN: 1-4107-0737-7 (Paperback)

Library of Congress Control Number: 2002096822

This book is printed on acid free paper.

Printed in the United States of America
Bloomington, IN

1stBooks – rev. 01/24/03

A No-Nonsense, Straightforward Discussion of Management Accounting Tools & Techniques That Will Sharpen Your Decision-Making Skills

Dedication

This book is dedicated to my grandmother, "Nettie" Dignam, without whose love and support my life would have been quite different, and not for the better.

Table of Contents

Introduction

Cavemen had it made; their decision-making was simple. Should I club a mastodon or stone a saber-toothed tiger? Then some clown got the bright idea that it might make sense to quantify the answers to those questions so he began to move small piles of rocks around and look to see which of the piles was the largest.

Next, someone in the Far East came up with another stroke of genius; why not put some holes in the stones and put them on rods in a little box? That way, the stones won't get lost, and so the abacus was born.

Somewhere along the line, the Romans showed up and they decided that the pile-of-rock system needed some improvement, so they called in a consultant. Of course the consultant was an MBA (that's code for "Marginally-Bright Advisor") who arrived at the brilliant scheme called Roman numerals. The fact that this system would require many, many, many weeks of employee training to implement had no bearing on the design of the system, of course. The Romans had received the name of the consulting firm from their auditors, which appeared to be wise because if you can't trust your auditor, whom can you trust? This project was completed around MDCCLXVII, BBC (Before Bankruptcy Court).

As a side note, if you are speaking with young people today do not talk about $50M, **M being the Roman symbol for 1,000**; they will not know that to which you make reference. Today you must use the term $50K, as in kilobyte. To the upcoming leaders of the world M means mega-something. I know from first hand experience while teaching at a university;

if I were to put Roman numerals on the blackboard , my accounting students might conclude that they were in a Chemistry Class and walk out.

Despite the fact that too many people seem to think of the people of the Middle East as having had nothing better to do during the past several hundreds of years than trying to kill one another, there apparently were a few people who were attempting to develop a method of recording numeric data in a fashion that would allow one to reach a conclusion prior to running out of writing fluid. Hence, the Arabic numbering system (you know, "1, 2, 3,..."). The system worked rather well, but it wasn't the end-all to beat all, because something was missing.

Then, late one Saturday night, or early Sunday morning, no one remembers for sure, since the group had been at the opium pipes for awhile, a big-mouthed academic-type pipes up, "We have developed a really cool counting system. I find absolutely NOTHING wrong with it."

Thanks to the Lord, his wife was in attendance at the gathering, and fulfilling her mission in life, she challenged the man's statement. "What do you mean NOTHING?" she asked. What is that supposed to mean, is that code for something?" (This all took place prior to zip codes and area codes, of course.)

His response was what one would expect it to be. "I think you may have had a bit too much to smoke, my dear! I said 'nothing' and I meant nothing!"

The Mrs. replied, "That isn't much of an answer, but I think I may be able to demonstrate exactly why 'NOTHING' is 'SOMETHING."

After the party finally broke up and the academic-type, with all of his degrees, and his spouse returned home to culminate the evening's socializing (it was a Saturday night) the Mrs. suddenly developed a severe headache and retired for the night. This was not the final scene that Dr. Knowsitall had in mind, and Mrs. Knowsitall knew it.

The following morning Mrs. Knowsitall asked her husband if he had enjoyed the previous evening's bash, and he replied that it sort of ended on a down note, like, NOTHING happened. She then asked "what do you mean nothing happened?" What she had in mind, she explained, was that if NOTHING happened then why should it have a depressing effect on one's perception of the events of the evening? It seems to me that if NOTHING can have some causal effect, NOTHING must be SOMETHING. The famous A. Knowsitall, Ph D, painfully and slowly began to absorb what his wife had said.

Upon waking, and during the commercial break of a camel race he was watching on ESPN (East Sinai Peninsula Network), he had a flash of brilliance, almost at the exact instance his dog, "Zero" lifted his leg to take a "whiz", causing the doctor scream out, "Zero, don't do anything, and I mean do NOTHING!" The light bulb lit up in Dr. Knowsitall's mind and he blurted out, "that's it, I understand that nothing is really something." In gratitude to his dog's contribution, Dr. Knowsitall decided to call "nothing" ZERO.

With the introduction of zero, the amount of data available and the gyrations through which the data could be driven grew exponentially, even though no one knew anything about exponents at the time.

Humankind's relentless search for ways by which one might accomplish more while doing less, also referred to as productivity, has compounded the growth-rate of information generation. Devices such as mechanical calculators, comptometers, and slide rules came first. Electrical and mechanical calculators, both of which led to computers, then followed.   Finally, with the invention of the "CHIP" as in computer-chip, not as in potato, the toll gates holding back the numbers were thrown open. Since that event took place, many careers, ideas, and a considerable amount of money have been lost.   Persons who were once thought to be competent and bright have found themselves lying at the side of the action wondering what it was that had run them over. "Did anyone get the name on the truck or its registration number?" they ask.

The purpose of this book is to assist the reader in dealing with the onslaught of ever-increasing reams of information and columns of numbers. Some grasp and understanding of what management accounting is all about, why and how its tools were developed, and how and when they should be used, will alert managers to the dangers that can arise from not having a feeling for the various concepts and techniques that are used in modern-day internal financial reporting and decision-making. Ignorance may be bliss, but I happen to think that it is the ignorance on the part of other people that brings bliss into my backyard.

Numbers or presentations of those numbers in various very "official" appearing formats must not intimidate you when making decisions. Accounting is not "hard science" and that means interpretation of accounting data leaves room for judgment.   Good judgment is one of the hallmarks of good decision-making. However, one is not in a position to render a sound opinion in the absence of some knowledge of that which is being judged. Try making a decision regarding the quality of play in a cricket match you have just watched on television in the middle of the night (you couldn't sleep because of the BIG MEETING in the morning). Unless you are from someplace like the United Kingdom or Australia, you haven't the foggiest idea of what poor or excellent play looks like. Are you aware, for example, that cricket is played on a round field?

Under those circumstances, how could you possibly render an intelligent opinion about the quality of the play? You might resort to the old, "If you can't dazzle them with brilliance, then you baffle them with bull s—, but that will only help you to survive for a relatively short period of time. One cannot just 'talk the talk' one must also be able to 'walk the walk." Either "you got game," or you don't.

After reading this book, you will be ready to deal with the numbers game, calculate the odds, and put the wagers that will determine your future success on the right horse. I am not promoting, condoning or badmouthing gambling here, but all of life is a gamble. Why not try to have the odds in your favor? Doing so is not mandatory, of course. One can always adopt the philosophy of the infamous Alfred E. Newman, of <u>Mad</u> magazine, "What, me worry?"

When possible, I will use everyday life activities to illustrate certain terminology. For example, when we discuss FIXED COSTS I will use one's apartment rent or home mortgage payment as an example of fixed cost. When we talk about VARIABLE COSTS I will show how the amount of money spent to purchase gasoline <u>varies</u> with the number of miles one drives an automobile. I believe this approach will enhance the reader's understanding of the information presented in this document.

Believe it or not, individuals and businesses have a great deal in common: Both need more income than outgo to survive. Both are striving to improve their economic positions. Both have fixed expense commitments. Both face unexpected changes in their economic environment. Both must make decisions that affect their futures, and both need meaningful information in order to make intelligent decisions. ACCOUNTING, IN ALL OF ITS BRANCHES, IS ABOUT PROVIDING INFORMATION TO DECISION-MAKERS, BOTH INDIVIDUALS AND BUSINESS LEADERS.

Sometimes, however, in the interest of being thorough, reporters of data can get carried away. That is, the quantity of data reported is so massive that it becomes both intimidating and confusing. This is true more than ever in our current age of technology. The personal computer and the internet are capable of generating enormous amounts of information in the wink of an eye. One of the key skills you must acquire is the ability to separate relevant information from facts and numbers that are of no consequence. If you are determined to go hunting on opening day, come hell or high water, all you want and need to know is, when is opening day. You are not interested in predictions about weather conditions, traffic conditions or the number of other hunters who will be in the field. Whatever those numbers indicate, you don't care; you are going hunting with your son on opening day, period!

As you read the following pages we expect that you will be quite surprised at the similarities between managing one's personal affairs and managing the affairs of a business. It often times is helpful to substitute personal decision-making issues for ones that are business-oriented. This personalization can help to clarify the issues and highlight the critical elements.

Dump your spouse or fire an employee? Both actions may lead to a lawsuit. Both actions may cost you a bundle of money in the future. Both may have been a mistake because the replacement was even worse than the one you ousted. Both are unpleasant tasks and both may have serious repercussions, but decisions must be made. That analogy may appear to be a bit flippant, but it isn't, and neither is management decision making! Unfortunately, or fortunately (depending upon whether you are from the glass half-full or glass half-empty school of thinking), decision-making is the heart and soul of being a manager.

When you have finished reading this book you WILL NOT be qualified to call yourself a management accountant. You should, however, be able to communicate intelligently with those persons who are qualified. It is likely that you will sound like you know that about which you speak, and that is important. Once the person on the other side of the table comes to realize that you know the score you can put away your snow shovel and hip boots because the likelihood of encountering a snow job or a BS barrage has been greatly diminished.

And so, let us begin.

"Ask not what the numbers can do for you;

Ask what you can do with the numbers!"

John F. Kennedy

Chapter 1

What Is Management Accounting?

Accounting, in general, is about communicating financial information in a format that allows the reader to draw conclusions, formulate opinions, and make decisions. Accounting is not "hard science," nor is it mathematics; it is a communications vehicle. There are two major branches of the subject: Financial Accounting and Managerial Accounting, the subject of this writing. The simplest way to understand what managerial accounting (a synonym for <u>management</u> accounting) is seems to be to compare it with financial accounting.

Financial Accounting is a highly structured system of communication, whose audiences are typically senior-level managers and entities external to the organization that have an economic interest in the financial health of the organization about whose operations financial reports are being published. These entities external to the organization are most often creditors, potential creditors, investors, and potential investors. The external entities are in need of information with which they may make financial resource allocation decisions: Should I lend money to this organization? Should I invest in this organization? Should I withdraw what I have previously invested in this organization? Was I out of my mind when I made that loan?

Financial Accounting reports of this type are the ones being discussed when one speaks about Enron, Global Crossing, Arthur Andersen, etc. Those debacles are the result of "outsiders" having made decisions based upon information

1

contained in published reports dealing with the financial condition and results of operations of the companies in which investments were made.

The answers to the above lending and investing questions are frequently formulated based upon the <u>past financial performance</u> of the organization under review, and that is what Financial Accounting is about, <u>the past</u>. Because these reports are related to past activity, their issuance must await completion of the period upon which the reports will be fashioned. That means a time delay, some times a delay of several months, before the needed information is forthcoming.

Managerial Accounting, on the other hand, is about the <u>future</u>. The questions aren't about what was done and what results were achieved, rather they are about what should be done now and what results we might expect to accomplish. Internal decision-makers are the persons who can most effectively answer those questions. To do so, however, necessitates the availability of timely information about present conditions and assumptions and estimates of what the future may hold for the organization. Therefore, timeliness of the data available is crucial to management accounting. A delay of several months in receiving information, which is often the case with financial accounting reports, is just not acceptable for managerial accounting purposes. This demand drove the development of the concept that numbers "in the ballpark" are acceptable for use in managerial accounting.

When making economic resource-allocation decisions, both creditors and investors are faced with choosing among a number of alternatives. Primarily, these choices involve financing (lending or investing) with Company A, Company B, or some other entity. That decision-making process is not unlike what we experience when contemplating the purchase of an automobile; should we purchase a Ford or a General Motors product? The intelligent investor or purchaser immediately wants to compare Choice A with Choice B. To do so the decision-maker must gather data about each of the items to be compared, one against the others.

Of course, comparing data can only give fruitful results if the data to be compared are comparable. That is, the data must include the same benchmark-data and the data must have been assembled in exactly the same manner. We are all aware of the fallacy of "comparing apples with oranges."

The information needs of persons interested in financial accounting information are rather similar and that makes it possible to establish a set of rules to follow when assembling reports for these users. An entity named the Financial Accounting Standards Board (FASB, pronounced "FASBIE") has done just that. The set of rules is called Generally Accepted Accounting Principles (GAAP, pronounced "GAP," like the clothing retailer by the same name). Because of GAAP users of financial accounting reports can feel somewhat comfortable, or at least one time they could, that they are, in fact, comparing apples to apples when looking at the data from company A and company B. That is referred to as comparability of data.

The rules of GAAP are very specific and leave little room for reformulating information to meet the needs of different circumstances. Given the rigidity of the rules there is not much opportunity for the rewriting of history to suit the needs of the publishers of financial accounting reports. Certified Public Accountants are often engaged to review financial accounting reports and to attest to the fact that the GAAP rules were followed appropriately. Unfortunately, there have apparently been some breaches of the attestation standards in recent times. Hopefully, like financial accounting, that sort of behavior will also become historic in nature.

Internal users of financial information, however, are faced with a different set of problems and circumstances within which decisions must be made. You the reader face the same type of problem. Again, if you are considering purchasing an automobile, you probably don't care what the cost of an automobile was last year; you want to know what the cost is today. Furthermore, you will want to know what the cost of insurance premiums might be, based upon different insurance-coverage combinations, or what the finance charges will be over various loan periods.

In such a situation, you need decision-specific information. That is you want to know the price of the vehicle, the costs of various insurance plans, and the interest rates for various financing options. These data are described as being relevant information. From a decision-making perspective, information is only relevant if it will have an effect on the events of the future. To accommodate these needs, managerial accounting has basically done away with rules regarding information presentation. The only master rules are that the information presented must be related to the decision under consideration, and it must be timely. This stance permits managerial accounting to be very flexible and innovative.

KEY CONCEPT:

Management accounting information must be relevant to the decision-making process for the problem at hand, and it must be available NOW!

We need to call to the mind of the reader that when we are discussing financial accounting reports and managerial accounting reports we are discussing financial information that comes from the same database. There are not two sets of books. Nevertheless, different assumptions and accounting techniques may be and often are used for completing income tax returns. Whether information is managerial or financial in nature depends upon the use to which the information will be put.

In general, how do management accountants work with the data at hand? Let's proceed and find an answer to that question.

There was a manager who lived in a shoe. She had so many numbers she didn't know what to do. And that's why she could afford only to live in a shoe!
Mother Goose?

Chapter 2

What Are The Skills
Managers Should Master?

Managers must first master the meaning of certain terms widely used in the profession. The first of these terms that we will consider is **cost structure**. All entities, both individuals and businesses, have a combination of cost-inputs and it is that combination which defines an entity's unique cost structure. The cost-inputs are divided into two classes; **fixed costs**, and **variable costs**.

When one defines something as being either fixed or variable the definition must include a comparison to something; there must be a reference point. We all understand that "fixed," means something similar to inert, unchanging, or rigid. The building you are occupying while reading this is attached permanently to the earth. Unless there is an earthquake or a super explosion, it is not moving. Therefore, if our reference point is the earth, its position is fixed. However, the earth is orbiting around the sun, which means that if the solar system is our point of reference, the building is not fixed.

The word 'variable' brings to mind the concept of something that is changing, or at least something that is subject to change. The temperature in the building in which you find yourself is subject to change. It may be warmer on sunny days than it is on days that are overcast. The temperature may be higher or lower depending upon the extent that heating or air conditioning devices are employed. Variability must also be measured against some standard. Let's assume that we set the standard at 72 degrees Fahrenheit. We are now able to read the thermometer at various intervals to see if the current temperature has varied from the standard with some degree of accuracy. We can say more than "it's hotter" or "it's cooler," we can state precisely how much hotter or cooler it has become.

The standard by which cost-inputs are determined to be either fixed or variable in managerial accounting is by comparing those items to some measuring stick, and that device is generally the volume of production for the period under examination.

There are some variations to the basic concepts of "fixed" and "variable," but we will leave that until later.

It is important for managers to make these comparisons, because by doing so, the managers are able to draw conclusions about how costs will behave (change or not change) in response to changes in production or sales volumes or both. No one is able to change the past, and so the conclusions drawn relate to volume changes that may occur in the future, which should be the focus of managers' activities.

Earlier it was stated that all of the information used in both financial and managerial accounting is gathered from the same source; no two sets of books are maintained. The use to which the data is put determines whether it is managerial in nature or financial in nature.

It should be added here that the same data may be characterized as being fixed or variable. Once again the definition is driven by the context in which the information is being studied. For example, a male human being may be characterized as being a father, a husband, an uncle, a brother, etc. If I am talking about uncle John or your brother John or your sister-in-law's husband John, I am referring to the same person.   Similarly, if I am talking about the fixed cost of electricity or manufacturing overhead or the unit fixed cost of production I am talking about the same invoice from the supplier of electrical power.

KEY CONCEPT:

**Managers must understand
cost behaviors.**

**Lord give me the serenity to accept the numbers I
cannot change,
the courage to change the numbers I can change,
and the wisdom to be able to recognize the difference**
Dr. Reinhold Niebuhr

There are many more terms and concepts with which managers must be familiar, but before we get to those let's take a quick look at an example of how knowing the differences between fixed and variable costs should be used in the decision-making process.

Let's assume that you are considering opening a storefront pizza business. In order to do so, you will need to rent space, purchase equipment, purchase insurance, obtain a license from the health department, and spend money to advertise this new venture.   THESE ARE THE FIXED COSTS of beginning the business. The costs will be the same if you sell one pizza or 1,000 pizzas.

You will also have to purchase the ingredients with which the pizzas will be made and the paper supplies for packaging the pizzas. Additionally, you will need to employ people to take orders, make pizzas and perhaps a person to deliver pizzas.

THESE ARE THE VARIABLE COSTS. The more pizzas you make and sell the more of the variable costs you will incur.

Given the fact that you think you want to go into the business of making and selling pizzas we can jump to the conclusion that you want to do so for the purpose of enhancing your wealth (making a profit). A fundamental question, then, is how many pizzas you will need to sell in order to generate the profits you seek. An understanding of the behavior of costs will go a long way toward answering that question, and perhaps avoiding a disaster similar to the one that follows.

I had a client once who operated a very successful specialty retail operation. We will call him "Adam" to protect the guilty. Adam decided that if he was making money operating at one location, he could make at least twice as much money if he opened a second location. Adam was never one to let facts get in the way of moving ahead with his plans, and as a matter of fact resented being asked questions such as, "Are you sure this is going to work? Have you thought about this?"

After finding a location and committing himself to a five-year lease with a personal guarantee of the rent payments. That means Adam had just put himself on the hook for $300,000 (12 months @ $5,000 times 60 months). Next, significant investments were made in designing and furnishing the interior of the rented property, much of those furnishings permanently attached to the structure. When items are attached to a rented structure those items become the property of the landlord.

Inventories were ordered and employees were then hired, including a manager and an assistant manager who were both salaried employees. Salaries are generally put into the fixed costs basket. All was then in place and ready to go.

A grand opening was held and it was promoted via significant print and radio advertising. And guess what happened; very few customers showed up. Not only was the grand opening a disappointment, the volume of customers coming into the store in the following weeks and months was also disappointing. The operation lasted five months, and Adam ended up in the hospital being treated for severe depression.

Had Adam made an analysis of his fixed and variable costs and from that analysis determined what volume of sales it would take to at least break even he might have saved himself a great deal of grief, not to mention the savings of all those fixed-costs committed dollars.

Adam was looking backward and using financial accounting data instead of looking forward and using managerial accounting data and tools.

After a few years, Adam came up with another grand plan for expansion. I began to ask hard questions regarding planning and assumptions regarding the new venture. Adam didn't like that, and he fired me.

Let's assume that your fixed costs, as enumerated above, will total $3,000 per month. Keep in mind that because these costs are FIXED COSTS the total will be $3,000 per month regardless of the number of pizzas you sell, or do not sell. Let's further assume that you are not interested in making the same mistakes that our friend Adam made.

Calling to mind the fact that **total cost** consists of two elements, the fixed part and the variable part, you now need to find the dollars that will be consumed by the variable costs elements (ingredients, preparation/delivery labor and packaging). Assume that these variable costs will amount to four dollars per pizza created and sold. Additionally we will take the position that the going-price for a pizza in your market area is nine dollars. You are now in a position to use management accounting to answer the question, "How many pizzas will I have to sell each month if I want to be successful?"

The first thing to consider is the fixed cost. If one can't pay that $3,000 each month, there is no way one is going to earn a profit. Just managing to pay the fixed cost is called the **breakeven point.** If one cannot break even there is certainly no room for making a profit. You now need to learn another management accounting term: **contribution margin** (also referred to as the gross profit).

The contribution margin per unit is the selling price of a unit of product less the variable cost for one unit of product. In your pizza business the unit contribution margin is $5.00. That is, a selling price of $9.00 less the variable costs of $4.00 for one pizza. The contribution margin may also be expressed as a percentage of the selling price; in the case at hand, the contribution-margin percentage (also referred to the contribution-margin ratio) is 55.6 per cent. Dividing the contribution margin per unit by the sales price per unit results in the percentage:

$$\$5.00/\$9.00 = 55.6\%.$$

Here are the questions and answers:

How many pizzas will I have to sell to break even?

$3,000 of fixed costs divided by a contribution margin of $5.00 per pizza indicates that 600 pizzas will have to be sold in a month if you are going to breakeven:

$$\$3,000/\$5.00 = 600 \text{ pizzas.}$$

However, one doesn't just want to break even, a profit of $1,200 per month appears to be the minimum needed to make the venture worthwhile. How many pizza sales will that require?

All one need do is add the desired profit to the total of the fixed costs and then do the same arithmetic to find the answer to that question:

($3,000 fixed costs + $1,200 desired profit) divided by $5.00 = 840 pizzas.

As the potential owner of the pizza business, you must now ask yourself the question, "Can I sell 840 pizzas each month?" If the answer is no, think of another opportunity to pursue. If the answer is yes, start looking for a location for the new business.

A second way to answer the "how much do I have to sell" question is to use the contribution-margin percentage method. Here is how it would be done for the same desired $1,200 profit question posed above:

Fixed costs of $3,000 plus desired profit of $1,200 equals $4,200.

$4,200 divided by the contribution margin percentage of 55.6 percent equals total sales of $7,554.

Total sales of $7,554 divided by $9.00 per pizza equals 839.3 pizzas.

($3,000 + $1,200) / .556 = $7,554

KEY CONCEPT:

Contribution margin is an essential element to be given consideration when dealing with "What if?" and "How much?" questions.

Measure twice and make the decision once, not the other way around
Anonimous

Chapter 3

A Further Look At The Fixed/Variable
Cost Concept

The tool that you have just encountered is a very early and basic use of the managerial accounting tool known as **CVP**, which is shorthand for **cost/profit/volume analysis**. It is a very powerful tool.

Let's assume that you want to increase the volume of sales in your new pizza business. To do so, you are thinking about launching a promotion campaign that is going to be comprised of two elements: advertising, and a give-away of a one-liter bottle of cola with each pizza a customer purchases from you. You have done your homework and have determined that the advertising campaign for bi-weekly ads over the next month will cost $600. Moreover, you have made a deal with a soft drink vendor to sell you one-liter bottles of cola for 75 cents each.

Before going ahead with the campaign, you would like some feel for what the sales volume should to be to make this a worthwhile venture. That question can be addressed using CVP analysis. Here we go:

Fixed costs have now increased to $3,600. (Original Fixed Cost of $3,000 plus the added $600 for the advertising portion of the campaign.) Variable costs per pizza sold have now grown to $4.75. (Original variable costs of $4.00 plus the cost of a liter of cola; $0.75 per liter.)

The contribution margin (**CM**) has declined to $4.25; the $9.00 selling price less the new variable cost of $4.75 per pizza.

Here is the answer of how many pizzas you will need to sell to reach breakeven:

Fixed costs of $3,600 divided by the REVISED CM of $4.25. The result is that a total of 847 pizzas will have to be sold to break even.

$$\$3,600 / \$4.25 = 847$$

The whole purpose of the campaign, of course, is to sell more pizzas so you can earn a larger profit. The $600 increase in fixed cost represents a twenty-percent increase. Given that fact, your desired increase in profits is also twenty-percent, or a $300 increase over the previous target-profit of $1,200. Therefore:

New Fixed cost ($3,600) plus new target profit ($1,500) divided by the new CM indicates that you will need total sales of 1,200, a volume increase of 43 percent:

$$(\$3,600 + \$1,500) / \$4.25 = 1,200 \text{ Pizza Sales}$$
See Exhibit 1.

Forty-three percent is a big number. Is it realistic? Can your present staff accommodate that growth or will you have to hire an additional employee? You need to answer these questions before you go forward. In the absence of a "quick and dirty" CVP analysis you may not be aware of the questions needing answers prior to your making a decision whether or not to proceed with your plan.

These types of analysis can also be done in graphic form where the graphic presentation allows you to look at the expected results over a range of sales volumes. See Exhibit #1

First a standard graph is created with sales volume in dollars on the left, the Y axis; and units of sales across the bottom, the X-axis.

A horizontal line is drawn across the graph to represent the total fixed costs.

Next we go to the upper–right-hand side of the graph and mark a point where sales volume at the contemplated unit sales price is found. A line is then drawn from that point downward and to the left corner that represents zero sales in units and zero sales in dollars.

The final step is to find a point on the vertical line that was used to plot total sales revenue in the step described above. This point should be the product of the total number of units sold multiplied by the unit variable cost. A line is then scribed from that point downward and to the left. However, the line is not downward sloped to the zero point, as was the case with the revenue-line. The y-axis intercept for this line is the point at which the fixed-cost line touches the Y axis.

How does one read the graph?

All along the line we have drawn to represent variable cost, we have a **total cost line**. That is because the line represents the total of fixed cost plus total variable cost at various sales volumes.

At the point where the total-cost line intersects with the total-revenue line is the breakeven point. The total revenue at this point is equal to the sum of total fixed costs plus total variable costs at that sales volume.

Note that if we use our imagination we can see an "X" growing out of the breakeven point. The widening space of the "X" above the point of breakeven represents profits. On the other hand, the widening space in the "X" below the breakeven point represents losses.

Breakeven graphs are easily constructed with the various computer spreadsheet programs available today. To play the "what if" game, simply vary the input numbers and see what happens.

In the process of constructing the graph three basic assumptions were made:

1. The total fixed cost would not change.
2. The variable cost per unit sold would remain unchanged.
3. The selling price per unit would remain constant at $9.00 per pizza.

We must make these assumptions in order to make predictions about what will happen at various sales levels. As long as these assumptions hold true, we can plan for the future. If any of these factors change, we have to return to the drawing board and make some new assumptions.

For example, if you are able to make and sell any number of pizzas between one and 2,000 per month in your existing facilities, the total fixed cost will remain the same. Once you move beyond a volume of 2,000 pizzas per month you will need to expand your facilities and your fixed costs will increase in total. The span of volume between one and 2,000 pizzas, the span in which your assumptions about revenue/costs behavior are valid is called the **relevant range.**

KEY CONCEPT

Assumptions involving the behavior of revenues and costs are only valid within the relevant range.

Last week I ordered an entire meal in French; even the waiter was surprised; it was a Chinese restaurant
(language outside of the relevant range)
Henny Youngman

Chapter 4

CVP and Product-Mix Decisions

As pointed out in the previous chapter, CVP analysis is a powerful tool that can be helpful in many decision-making situations. Here is another example of how you can put this tool to work for you.

Among other items, your pizza establishment menu includes "Sausage Pizza" and "Pepperoni Pizza," both of which sell for the same $9.00 price. However, because of pepperoni's strong taste it requires only one-fourth of a pound of meat whereas the sausage pizza takes one-half pound of meat. Both ingredients are purchased for $2.40 per pound from the meat purveyor from whom you purchase your supplies.

	SAUSAGE	PEPPERONI
Menu Price	$9.00	$9.00
Meat Cost	(1.20)	(.60)
Other Costs	(2.80)	2.80)
Contribution Margin	$ 5.00	$ 5.60

Clearly, pepperoni pizzas are more profitable, as a matter of fact, 6.7 per cent more profitable. Therefore, it would seem to make sense for you to "push" pepperoni pizzas with some type of promotion. Let's see what might happen if you decide to feature pepperoni pizzas at a special price of $8.50.

First we will assume that you are selling 1,200 pizzas each accounting period, 30 percent pepperoni and 70 percent sausage. What happens to the bottom line if the new pricing converts one-third of the sausage buyers into pepperoni buyers?

	SAUSAGE	PEPPERONI	TOTALS
630 pizzas X $9.00	$5,670		
570 pizzas X $8.50		$4,845	
			$10,515
Variable Costs			
630 X $4.00	2,520		
570 X $3.40		1,938	4,458
Contribution Margin	$3,150	$2,907	$6,057
Fixed Costs			3,000
Net Income			**$3,057**

Operating Results Before The Price Promotion:

1,200 pizzas @ $9.00	$10,800
Variable Costs	4,584
Contribution Margin	$ 216
Fixed Costs	3,000
Net Income	**$ 3,216**
Original Net Income	$3,216
Promotion-Driven Net Income	3,057
Decrease in Net Income	**$ 159**

Well, it's back to the drawing board. You want to increase, not decrease net income. Actually, you could have stopped the moment you saw that the total contribution margin for the original pricing ($4,584) was greater than the total contribution margin of the revised pricing ($4,458).

An even shorter approach would be to multiply the per-unit contribution margin by the expected sales volumes:

Sausage Pizza	630 X $5.00	$3,150
Pepperoni Pizza	570 X $5.10	$2,907
		$6,057
Original Contribution Margin		6,216
Loss of Contribution Margin		($ 159)

Once the breakeven point has been reached every dollar of additional contribution margin falls directly to the net income line. Therefore, beyond the breakeven point, any schemes that increase contribution margin should be pursued, and those that do not should be abandoned.

Well, you have used CVP analysis to test two marketing ideas and neither of them seemed promising. The first increased the total contribution by so little that taking the risk of assuming the added cost of advertising and the expense of the soft drinks to give away just wasn't worth it.

All attempts to increase income fall somewhere on the risk/reward curve. The risk/reward curve presents in graphic form the dollars that might be gained in relationship to the risk to be assumed. The greater the risk one is willing to assume the greater the return one is entitled to receive.

If you happen to be at a thoroughbred track and are considering making a two-dollar wager you are facing a risk/reward decision. Do you bet your two dollars on the favorite that is likely to go off at even money and collect $4.00 if that horse wins? Or do you lay your wager on a horse with fifty-to-one odds and pick up $100 if the horse comes in first?

You face similar decisions in business. Should you invest excess funds in U. S. Government securities and earn four percent, or purchase corporate "junk bonds" with a promised yield of twelve percent?

More specifically, are you willing to invest an additional $600 for advertising and another $400+ for soft drinks to promote additional sales that MAY yield an added $300 in profits?

The second plan to increase profits by shifting the balance of the product mix toward pepperoni pizzas was even worse. An analysis of that plan suggested that you would actually decrease profits by $159 if that plan were implemented. If you decide to go ahead with that plan anyway, save yourself some time and aggravation. Open the cash register, take out $159 and give it to your favorite charity. Or, use the $159 for a few visits to your local headshrinker.

There you stand with two less–than-ideal ideas; you have two strikes against you. But as Yogi Berra, a member of the Baseball Hall of Fame, and perhaps remembered even more for his ability to bat the English language around, once said, "It ain't over 'till it's over." Another person is reputed to have uttered, "It ain't over until the fat lady sings." It takes three strikes to be called out, and that means you still have a chance.

And the "fat lady" may be the chance you have been seeking. You can see it now: **LOW-CAL PIZZA!** Paraphrasing the late Dean Martin, **WHEN THE MEAL MISSES YOUR THIGHS LIKE LOW-CAL PIZZA PIES, THAT'S AMORE!** "It's a beautiful thing."

After some careful research, you learn that the ingredients required to make a quality pizza using things such as lowered-carbohydrate flour, reduced-fat mozzarella cheese, and tomato sauce with artificial sweeteners is almost identical to what you are currently using. It is now time for you to do another, "quick and dirty" CM analysis.

From the above analysis, it looks like it made some sense to take those first two pitches. This plan looks like it may have the potential to be an extra-base hit.

Management's time is valuable. By using the contribution margin tools available, eliminating unworkable projects, campaigns, etc. can be done quite quickly, but with a rather high degree of comfort.

KEY CONCEPT

Utilize available & tested shortcuts whenever possible when evaluating courses of action.

"Four score and seven years ago, our Fathers..."
Keep it simple; I think he meant
"About 87 years ago..."
Abraham Lincoln

Chapter 5

Making Scarce Resource Utilization Decisions To Maximize Profits

We will now move away from your pizza business and enter the factory of the manufacturer from whom you purchased your pizza-crust making equipment, Reno's Equipment Sales, Inc.

Reno's manufactures two types of crust-making equipment: The standard model and the deluxe model, and has a maximum capacity of 2,000 crust-making machines per month. Pricing and cost data for the two models is as follows:

	Standard Model	Deluxe Model
List Selling Price	$500	$800
Variable Costs	$300	$500
Contribution Margin	$200	$300

The major component of the machines is stainless steel, and both models require five pounds of stainless steel. However, because of its complexity, the deluxe model requires four hours of assembly-technician time, versus just two hours of assembly for the standard model. Technicians earn $25.00 per hour. including fringe benefits and payroll taxes, at straight-time rates. Any overtime pay will increase the cost to $37.50 per hour of production.

24

For the purpose of protecting American steel producers, the federal government recently imposed import tariffs on foreign steel firms and that has caused a shortage of stainless steel.

Other manufacturers are experiencing similar steel-availability problems, creating an almost unlimited demand for crust-making equipment.

The dilemma faced, of course, is how to utilize the available labor hours most advantageously while avoiding the brutal cost of overtime pay.   In other words, what should be the production mix between standard and deluxe models? At first glance, it would appear that production of the deluxe model should win the day, because it has a contribution margin that is 150 percent of the contribution margin earned on the standard model.

What one must do to deal with this dilemma is calculate the **contribution margin per unit of the scarce resource**. The standard model requires two hours of labor to produce $200 of contribution margin. The deluxe model requires four hours of labor to produce $300 of CM. Therefore, it makes more sense, profit-wise, to produce the standard model even though it produces less CM per unit of finished product. Let's look at the numbers.

3,600 hours of labor will produce 1,800 standard machines.
3,600 / 2 = 1,800 Machines

3,600 hours of labor will produce 900 deluxe machines.
3,600 hours / 4 = 900 Machines

Therefore:
(3,600 / 2) X $200 = $360,000

VS
(3,600 / 4) X $300 = $270,000

If the strategy of devoting all of the scarce resources to the production of standard-model machines is adopted, the total contribution margin will be greater by $90,000 than if one jumped to the conclusion that the deluxe model should be produced because that model has a larger unit contribution margin.

Or
$360,000 Of CM / 3,600 = $100.00 Per Hour
Versus
$270,000 of CM / 3,600 = $75.00 Per Hour

Exhibit 2

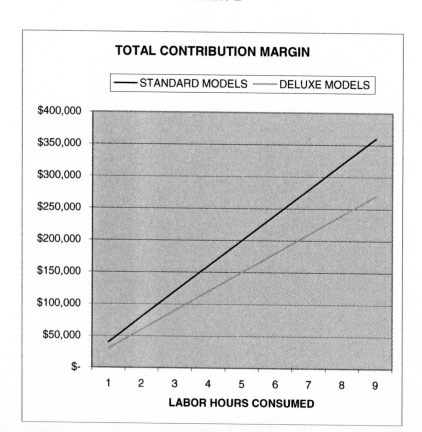

What if the scarce resource happens to be direct material?

The process is the same. Find the contribution margin per unit of scarce resource, and let that be your guide. However, you must be careful here. After all, it is the marketplace that determines what your product-mix and production volumes should be. When working with labor as the scarce resource, the assumption was made that there was unlimited demand, the ideal situation. Of course, that rarely is the case, unless you happen to be in the business of selling tickets to the Super Bowl Game; assuming they are not bogus tickets, congratulations.

Take a look at a more realistic situation:

Your pizza establishment has two menu items aimed at families in which both parents work; you offer the family-sized pizza and the family pasta dinner. Both of these items are profitable, although the contribution margin on the pasta dinner is a bit more attractive.

Due to an upheaval in the Italian Government, the umpteenth since the end of World War II, your ability to obtain quality ingredients has been curtailed. You refuse to lower the quality of your product and that means there may have to be some reduction in sales volume. What do you do? See Exhibit #3

Do an analysis of contribution margin per unit of your scarce resources to aid you in the decision of which menu items you should feature.

```
┌──────────────────────────────────────────────────────────────────────┐
│ Exhibit 3                                                              │
│                                                                        │
│          UTILIZATION OF SCARCE RESOURCE                                │
│          CONTRIBUTION MARGIN PER UNIT ANALYSIS                         │
│                                                                        │
│                                     FAMILY              FAMILY         │
│                                     PIZZA               MEAL           │
│          Selling Price           $    2.00           $    20.00        │
│                                                                        │
│          Variable Costs          $    5.00           $    10.00        │
│                                                                        │
│          Contribution Margin     $    7.00           $    10.00        │
│                                                                        │
│          Pounds of ingredients required    2                3          │
│                                                                        │
│          Contribution   margin   per   $   3.50     $      3.33        │
│          pound                                                         │
└──────────────────────────────────────────────────────────────────────┘
```

	FAMILY PIZZA	FAMILY MEAL
Selling Price	$ 2.00	$ 20.00
Variable Costs	$ 5.00	$ 10.00
Contribution Margin	$ 7.00	$ 10.00
Pounds of ingredients required	2	3
Contribution margin per pound	$ 3.50	$ 3.33

The above analysis suggests that the Family Pizza is the item that should be featured until the ingredient supply can recover. The reason? Because the contribution margin for the Family Pizza will put more dollars on the bottom line, where it counts.

Let's bring the concept of maximizing contribution margin in the face of scare resources into the home setting.

Your step-son, Dwart Farquart, is in his senior year of high school. He is a bright young man, but, unfortunately, during the past three and one-half years seems to have been majoring in the geography of the local shopping malls. He doesn't seem to know where one might find the Mount Rushmore Monument, or the names of the presidents whose images are depicted thereon, but just ask him where the nearest Banana Republic store is. You will learn the name of the shopping mall, the location of the store within the mall, and the hours of operation. You likely will also learn the name of the "hottest" sales clerk working there and what her hours of work are at the present time.

His grades, except for his course in sociology where an in depth study of the life-style of mall rats was undertaken, are atrocious. That not withstanding, he has recently informed you and your spouse that he thinks he is going to enroll in college. He is not sure yet where he might apply, but he is thinking about the University of Minnesota, given its proximity to the Mall of America. When you pose the question, "What about a major?" He responds that he isn't interested in the Reserve Officers Training Corps (ROTC) so he doesn't think a major is in the cards.

You realize, of course, that even with your gift of gab, there is no way this person is going to be accepted at a first-tier university. Your suspicions are confirmed when Dwart shows you some envelopes that have been addressed to a few top-notch schools and have been returned stamped "Addressee Unknown." A close examination of these envelopes gives you the impression that at least a few of the envelopes have been steamed open and re-sealed.

Your next move was to meet with his school counselor to discuss the situation. That meeting proved to be of little help, not that it was the counselor's fault. She was rather quiet, but quite polite. Not once did she burst into laughter or break down and cry.

Your managerial decision analysis skills are brought into play and you conclude that there are two courses of action available to you:

1. On Dwart's next mall excursion you pack the household furnishings, move out and do not leave a forwarding address.
2. Dwart can enroll in a school of lesser stature and attempt to establish an academic record that might result in his being accepted at a more prestigious institution of higher learning at some time in the future.

After what appeared to be a rather agonizing period of contemplation, your wife concludes that she can't support Option Number One, tempting as it sounded at first blush.

Given Dwart's performance over the past three and one-half years you believe getting him committed, I mean admitted, will require some serious research. Having done your homework it appears that another two options require a decision:

1. He attends East Overshoe University, which is located in the upper peninsula of Michigan, at a cost of $10,000 per year, or
2. He enrolls at We-Take-Anybody-Community College at a cost of $5,000 per year.

This is clearly an allocation of scare resources problem. Cash, of course, is always a scare resource. There is another scare resource with which you must also deal, that being the amount of actual intellectual input you might reasonably expect from Dwart.

But let us not be too hard on the lad. Let's, for argument sake, assume that the boy has actually seen the light, the light at the end of the tunnel leading to a college degree, not the light being reflected from the eyebrow ring worn by the Banana Republic store clerk. If that is indeed the case, and Dwart carries the normal full-load of classes, his input should be about 500 hours of work each academic year. You are interested in getting the most bang for your buck (pay attention, we are not talking about a night on the town with your buddies) so you sit down and run the numbers.

At East Overshoe University the input is 500 hours at a total cost of $10,000; $20 per hour of input for an output of 30 hours of credit.

At We-Take-Anybody-Community College the figures are $5,000 with the same input and that computes to $10 per hour while the output remains unchanged. When working with the effective utilization of scare resources there are two perspectives: More output with the same input, or the same output with less input. The latter of those two is the case here. It is quite clear that the local community college makes more sense from a review of the numbers.

A bit later in this book we will discuss considerations other than the ones that are strictly numeric in nature, and their importance in the decision-making process.

Here, briefly, is an example of thinking about the non-numeric issues involved in making a decision:

If Dwart enrolls in the community college he will, in all likelihood, be living at home. That means having him wandering through the house with the cd player blasting or boisterously cheering himself for his major coup in the computer game he has been playing via your telephone line for the past six hours. Moreover, it is very likely that Bambi, Tammy or Sandi, whatever the Banana Republic clerk's name is, will also be chilling out in your once peaceful abode. And like it or not, you will have to feed your son, and the occasional guests of his. (One meal per day is the definition of occasional when it comes to teenagers.) There is more, as you must realize, but I think the point regarding non-cash considerations has been made. Perhaps the added $5,000 to be able to root for the East Overshoe Onions (the name onions, frequently associated with things that stink, has absolutely nothing to do with the nickname adopted by the university's athletic department) doesn't look too bad after all.

But, "wait," you say, "I ran the numbers and the optimal decision here is quite clear." I had a feeling from the outset that the answer would clearly be to unload Dwart on, "ah," enroll the young scholar at the local community college. And your intuition was correct. Intuition is a very valuable asset and one that should always be given some consideration. Running the numbers is an adjunct to, not a replacement for exercising your judgment. You will find that being run over by the numbers can be caused by, 1. Failure to give the pertinent numbers any consideration, or, 2. Relying totally on what the numbers tell you.

KEY CONCEPT

Contribution Margin is key, but not the last word when dealing with scarce resource decisions.

To pay the extra $5,000 or not to pay the $5,000, that is the question.
"Wether tis nobler in the mind to suffer" the rap music and endless busy signal as I telephone home, or to bail out and blow a few bucks (not to mention maintaining my sanity), that is the question.
William Shakespeare

Chapter 6

Does It Make A Difference?

Does what make a difference? Does including all or just a portion of the costs in your decision-making process make a difference? It turns out that the answer is yes and no. Recall that decision-making affects the future, not the past. If the decision you are about to make will have an effect on some cost element's behavior in the future, that cost element **must** be part of the data under study. If any of those cost elements will be unchanged as a result of your decision, they should be excluded from the data being studied. If a cost element will remain unchanged despite the decision you make, that cost element is irrelevant to the decision at hand. It is not a **RELEVANT COST.**

In an earlier chapter, you looked at the idea of running a promotion to boost sales volume. The deal included a free liter of soft drink with the purchase of a pizza. You thought of spending $600 to advertise the promotion. In that case the added cost of the soft drinks (a variable cost), and the added $600 advertising expenditure (a fixed cost), would both change future expenditures. It follows then, because they would be different in the future than they are now, both are relevant to the decision of whether or not you should run the promotion.

On the other hand, when you looked at the problem of what mix of deluxe and standard model pizza-crust makers to produce, you ignored the fixed overhead data. That is because the overhead expense was going to be the same regardless of what production decisions were made. The overhead cost was not relevant in that instance because it was not an avoidable cost.

Each decision will involve a different mix of relevant and irrelevant data. But in all instances, whenever a cost element will be the same regardless of the decision that is made, that cost element is irrelevant to the decision at hand. The cost elements that will remain unchanged are referred to as **unavoidable costs.** All unavoidable costs are irrelevant to the decision making process.

Here is an example from a non-business perspective. Your oldest daughter, Susan, has recently agreed to marry the geek you can't stand. Nevertheless, you and your spouse have agreed to pay for the wedding reception. Projected costs are as follows for an expected 200 guests:

Live Music	$ 2,000
Hall Rental	1,000
Plated, sit-down meal	10,000
Call brand, open bar	4,000
Flowers & Candles for head table	500
Self-serve, buffet dinner	5,000
Limo from church to hall	150
Champagne with meal	300
Guest table name cards	100
Bar service for cash bar	400
Wine served with dinner	700
Bribe money to foster elopement	5,000

Having read the list, and shortly after the two of you regain consciousness, you begin the discussion of what to do. You decide that knowing the cost-per-guest will help you reach a decision.

Per-Guest Cost – 200 Guests

	Total	Sit-Down	Buffet
Hall Rental	1,000	1,000	1,000
Plated, sit-down meal	10,000	10,000	
Call brand, open bar	4,000	4,000	
Head table Decorations	500	500	500
Self-serve, buffet dinner	5,000		5,000
Limo from church to hall	150	150	150
Champagne with meal	300	300	
Guest table name cards	100	100	100
Bar service for cash bar	400	400	
Wine served with dinner	700	700	
Bribe money to foster elopement	5,000	5,000	5,000
Totals	$29,150	$23,450	$14,450
Cost Per Guest		$117.75	$72.75
Difference		$ 45.00	

All of the cost elements have been arrayed for your review. However, not all of the listed data are relevant to your decision; only the items that differ as a function of the decision that is made are relevant. We will now list only the avoidable costs to simplify the process.

Per-Guest Relevant Cost – 200 Guests

	Sit-Down	Buffet
Food	$10, 000	$5,000
Beverages	4, 000	400
Dinner Beverages	700	300
Totals	$14, 700	$5,700
Per Guest Costs	$73.50	$28.50
Difference	$45.00	

35

What we have done in the second instance is to separate the cost elements into **relevant** and **non-relevant** categories. That step simplifies the decision-making process. The cost elements that will **not** differ, based upon the decisions you make, are not relevant. Therefore, you can set aside the cost of the hall, the flowers, the limo, the guest cards, the music, and perhaps the bribe money. (You will spend the $5,000 as a wedding gift anyway.) These will be the same, regardless of what other choices are made.

That leaves the relevant costs elements: Sit-down meal or a buffet? Open bar or cash bar? Champagne or wine with dinner? Still not a pretty picture, but at least you have fewer numbers with which to become aggravated.

And, the fewer bits of data that one has to look at when trying to make a decision, the more likely it is that a sound decision will be made. Too much data can cause confusion and lead to misinterpretations of the facts.

On the other hand, too little or an incorrect reading of what data are relevant can also lead to errors. Try the following to estimate your remaining life-span:

Write down the first three numbers of your Social Security Number
Mine numbers are 3,1 and 8.
If you are a male subtract 2, if female, add 1
I am a male: 318 less 2 = 316.
Reverse those numbers. 316 reversed = 613
Subtract the smaller from the larger number. 613 − 316 = 297
Add the numbers left to right> 2 + 9 + 7 = 18
Divide the total by 2, 18 / 2 = 9

If you did the arithmetic correctly your answer is the same as mine, 9, and that is because the first three numbers of your Social Security Number are totally irrelevant in finding the answer to the question, "What is your remaining life span."

While on vacation at a dude ranch, your seven-year old son asks, "How many horses are in that pasture?" You have some options from which to choose: I don't know; make a wild guess; count the horses: count the horses' legs and divide by four; count the ears and divide by two, etc. The first choice might make you look incompetent in the eyes of your child. The second is being dishonest, and you do not want to instill bad habits in your son. The third makes sense, but it won't be easy. The fourth and fifth choices include information to process that is not relevant and only muddies up the task at hand, that is, IRRELEVANT DATA.

Being the astute manager that you are, you realize that this presents a learning opportunity for your child, and so you follow one of the cardinal rules of good management practice—you delegate and ask your son to do the counting and report back to you. The answer you will receive is probably going to be close enough for managerial decision-making purposes and you will not have wasted valuable time. You might first, however, explain the irrelevance of counting ears or legs.

Take another look at this technique, this time in a business setting.

Assume you are the general manager of a plant in which the pizza crust-making machines discussed earlier are manufactured. A cost report you have received shows the following cost analysis:

Cost Per 1,000 Units	Deluxe	Standard
Stainless Steel	$ 100,000	$ 100,000
Manufacturing Labor	100,000	50,000
Assembly Supplies	60,000	30,000
Equipment Wear & Tear	18,000	12,000
Factory Utilities	60,000	40,000
Plant Mgr. Salary	50,000	30,000
Supervisor Salary	25,000	15,000
Administrative Costs	87,000	23,000
Totals	$ 500,000	$ 300,000
Cost Per Unit	$ 500	$ 300

Costs other than material, labor and supplies are applied to the product lines based upon sales price. (In accountant-speak this is "applied overhead".) These are fixed costs. The equipment wear and tear costs are based upon the cost of a recently acquired specialty-machine that cost $30,000 and has no salvage value because it was engineered for just one use.

You have received a proposal from a machine-tool salesman to rent a piece of equipment that would replace the machine you recently purchased. The new machine is capable of reducing labor time by one hour per unit produced and it rents for $15,000 per year. Your initial reaction probably is that you just spent $30,000 for a new machine and the salesman is asking you to scrap it. What is wrong with this picture? Let's focus on the RELEVANT factors and find out.

Added cost of renting the machine	$15,000
Labor costs saved: 1 hour saved for each of the	
1,000 products manufactured @ $25 per hour:	$25,000
Profit improvement	$10,000

NONE of the other cost elements are relevant to this decision. Those costs will be incurred whether or not the new machine is rented.

But wait, what about the $30,000 that was just spent to purchase the first machine? That element is also irrelevant because the $30,000 has already been spent. Renting or not renting a new piece of equipment won't change that fact. The $30,000 is a **sunk cost** and sunk costs are never relevant, because they are now history and we cannot change the past. Our decisions deal with the future.

The charge for wear and tear on the equipment is referred to as **depreciation expense**. It is an accounting technique used to match expense with revenue, but the dollars involved have already been expended and may not be recouped. (Perhaps they can be in part, but only if the old equipment can be sold or traded.) One must be very careful when considering the numbers associated with depreciation. Because depreciation does not involve the consumption of cash it should be ignored in many situations, and if it isn't ignored, it is likely to lead to false conclusions.

One should readily appreciate the efficiency of working only with relevant data, as well as the clarity this decision-making technique brings to the task at hand.

The technique you have been looking at is called **relevant costing**. You may also hear people use the terms "**incremental costing**," or "**differential costing**." All three of these terms are basically interchangeable and all deal with what will change and by how much it will change, based upon the decision that is made.

Here is another example of the usefulness of relevant costing.

Once again you are the production manufacturer, this time in an organization that is **vertically integrated.** Your employer is a manufacturer of snowmobiles that require an alternator. Because of the firm's vertical integration the alternators are manufactured internally. The latest cost report for the production of the alternators shows the following for production-run of 10,000 units:

	Per Unit	Total
Manufacturing Labor	$ 15.00	$150,000
Identifiable Materials	20.00	200,000
Minor Supplies	3.00	30,000
Applied Overhead	6.00	60,000
Department Supervisor	4.00	40,000
Equipment Depreciation	12.00	120,000
Totals	$ 60.00	$ 600,000

A salesman representing a Taiwanese firm has approached the department manager and has made an offer to provide the alternators for $45 each. Do you accept the proposal?

The first step is to "blow away the smoke" (the cost elements that are not relevant to the decision at hand), you only want to consider the cost elements that are relevant. Those costs with which you should be concerned are the **AVOIDABLE COSTS.** What costs can be avoided, if you purchase rather than manufacturer the alternators?

Manufacturing Labor	$ 15.00
Identifiable Materials	20.00
Minor Supplies	3.00
Total Avoided	$ 38.00
Cost to Purchase	$ 45.00

What decision would you make? Even if you decide to "down-size" the department supervisor the numbers continue to lean toward continuing to build your own alternators.

KEY CONCEPT

Focus on how the equation will change because of the decision you make.

"A bird in the hand is worth two in the bush" Think it through before you decide to re-landscape.

Chapter 7

Other Considerations

The last chapter included the statement that the data "lean toward" continuing to manufacture the alternators. We used the term "lean toward" because "crunching numbers," as previously noted, in and of itself is rarely the final solution to the decision-making process. Other factors must be taken into consideration, and is why managers are paid to think.

Let's for the sake of illustration assume that, because of limited space, your firm is spending $84,000 per year to rent space for storage purposes. If you eliminate the manufacturing of alternators, the space used by that department could be converted to storage space. Now what?

Rent Expense Avoided	$84,000
Added cost of Purchasing Devices	
1,000 X $7.00	70,000
Difference	$14,000

Given this additional contribution margin, the option to purchase rather than manufacture the alternators looks more attractive.

What we are looking at is called an **opportunity cost.**

Opportunity costs are not recorded in the formal accounting records, but they **must never** be overlooked when making decisions. What exactly is an opportunity cost? Simply stated, it is the financial difference between choosing Option A over Option B. For example, purchase a $10,000 certificate of deposit @ 4 percent or put the $10,000 under your mattress (don't tell your spouse). The CD will earn you $400 in one year; the mattress will earn you zero (we are talking only in monetary terms here). The $400 is the opportunity cost of choosing the mattress over the CD investment.

Is that all there is to it? Not quite. There are always non-financial factors to take into consideration. When one switches to an out-side supplier for any item that becomes a part of the final product, some quality control is lost. Moreover, if you are buying parts from Taiwan and that country goes to war with China you are going to have one heck of a time trying to get the parts you need. If your supplier falls upon hard times and goes out of business, how long will it take you to gear up to begin producing the parts you need to complete your finished product again? Or, if there is an interruption in the transportation chain, such as a recent strike by dock workers, what might happen on your production line?

If organizations could operate just "by the numbers" successfully, they would do so. Computers are far less expensive than employees. Computers rarely get sick, they don't go on vacation, they don't play office politics, they don't have affairs with colleagues and they don't ask for raises. Fortunately, they don't think either. That is where you come in—the thinking part.

As one might imagine, there are many more instances wherein relevant costing, or differential cost analysis can be useful. Differential cost analysis can be applied to situations such as buy or lease; keep the old or buy a new car; travel by bus or travel by train, etc. However, we see little value in continuing to "beat a dead horse" by presenting an almost endless string of examples.

43

KEY CONCEPT

**After you crunch the numbers,
consider the other ramifications of your decisions.**

**I said to my mother-in-law, "my house is your house"
The next week she sold it!**
Henny Youngman

Chapter 8

Select A Point Of Attack

We'll take a break from most of the numbers for now and look at some general management decision-making concepts. The first thing we will introduce is the **Theory of Constraints**. The application of this principal is really common sense, but it is often ignored. Here is an example of the theory in action:

Return to the make/buy decision concerning the snowmobile alternators. The following relates to manufacturing steps and production capacities:

ACTIVITY	PRODUCTION CAPACITY
Stamp Housings	2,000 Per Month
Wind Armatures	1,800 Per Month
Create Wiring Assemblies	1,500 Per Month
Assemble Alternators	2,100 Per Month
Paint Alternators	3,000 Per Month

Question Number One; in the absence of inventories, what is the maximum number of alternators that can be produced in any one month? The answer, of course, is 1,500 because that is the maximum number of wiring assemblies that can be produced with the present capacity: This is the **constraint point**, a more academic sounding term for what we commonly refer to as a bottleneck.

What should be done if the production output is to be increased? The theory of constraints indicates that management's attention should be focused on the constraint point. Once that problem is addressed and remedied,

45

management should seek out the next "bottleneck." It is a continuous process.

In an earlier paragraph the phrase, "in the absence of inventories" was used, and that brings us to another resource control and utilization system, referred to as **JIT**. JIT is the acronym for **Just in Time** materials management.

Having inventories of raw materials, work in process and finished goods, all consume resources. Inventories tie up money that might be earning revenues in some other use. Insurance premiums must be paid to protect the resources that are in inventories. Inventories may actually decline in value due to damage, obsolescence or theft. Carrying inventories takes up space that might be put to some other productive use. Given these facts, it would seem to make managerial sense to eliminate or reduce to a minimum the amount of resources tied up in inventory.

That is the goal of JIT. Rather than purchase needed materials in large batches and have large quantities of items on hand, shipments arrive in more frequent, smaller quantities. Shipments come in when they are needed based upon a "pull" system of inventory management. Supplies are ordered and received as the production process creates demand for them. Suppliers are required to meet set standards regarding order size, delivery schedules, and quality assurance, for which they are generally rewarded with superior pricing.

It rarely happens, but this system should aim at an inventory turnover of 365 times per year: Material is received and used in just one 24-hour period. "In today, out tomorrow."

"In today and out tomorrow" relates to what is known as

THROUGHPUT TIME.

Throughput time is the time lapse between when raw material enters the production cycle and when it leaves the assembly line. Another term is **order processing time**. Here we tack on the time durations at the beginning of the cycle, the date the order is received, and when it goes into production, and the end of the cycle, which is the spread from finishing the production process and shipping the product to the customer.

Management's goal should be to reduce these time-spans to a minimum. The shorter these periods are, the fewer resources the firm has tied up in inventories. The approach to reducing throughput and order-processing time reduction is somewhat similar to dealing with the production-constraint problem. The first step is to array the activities involved:

ACTIVITY	TIME REQUIRED
Paperwork and scheduling	4 hours
Procedure 1 work	8 hours
Wait-time	8 hours
Procedure 2 work	9 hours
Relocation time	5 hours
Procedure 3 time	6 hours
Move time	5 hours
Shipping time	3 hours
Total order-processing time	48 hours

The second step is to identify which of these activities add value to the product and which ones do not. In this instance, paperwork, waiting, relocating, moving and shipping, although they are a part of the value chain, they add no value to the product. The breakdown is 23 hours of value-added time and 25 hours that do not enhance the value of the product.

The Ratio is: 23 hours Value-Added / 48 Total Hours = .48

The ideal is a ratio of 1 to 1. That is, all of the hours consumed are adding value to the product. That being the case, where should management focus its energies? Toward reducing non-value-added time, of course.

Bottlenecks, excess inventories, and excessive time devoted to activities that do not add value to the product present themselves as symptoms. These symptoms are visible manifestations of underlying problems. Just as a physician must observe symptoms and review other data in order to make a diagnosis of the problem, so must the successful manager reach a conclusion about the true nature of the underlying problem. Once the diagnosis is made a course of therapy (management actions) can be designed and implemented.

KEY CONCEPT

**Focus on the problem, not the symptoms,
then find a solution.**

**After my annual physical I asked my physician,
"Doc, how do I stand?"
The doctor replied,
"That's what puzzles me."**
Henny Youngman

Chapter 9

ABC

A Superior Diagnostic Tool

The pizza business has been going well, but because you are young and a Type A Personality you want to continue to grow the business. As you and your spouse walk toward your automobile after leaving a christening party for your niece, the "lightbulb" in your head turns on! The food served at the party was decent, but it wasn't of the same quality that you prepare in your place of business. That is not the point; the point is that the food was not homemade; it was **catered**.

Catering, that's the next growth opportunity for which you have been hunting. You are really excited, so you drop your spouse off at the house and head for your office at the shop. During the drive you make a firm decision that profits in the catering business must be at least equal to what you are currently generating on a per-serving basis.

Once you reach the office you quickly lay out the data as shown in the upper portion of Exhibit #4 The per-person-served pricing schedule you adopt indicates that the desired contribution can be obtained.

After some print advertising and word of mouth referrals from satisfied customers, the catering segment of the business begins to roll. As a matter of fact, it rolls so well that you are required to hire an employee to deal with the catering business and to purchase a delivery van. Trying to cram pizzas and dinners for 30 or 40 people into an automobile just doesn't cut it.

Some months have passed since the catering service was introduced and it is getting close to the time of the year when you must deal with Uncle Sam. A closer look at your current cash situation brings you up short. You may be in the prepared food business, but your question is not, "Where's the beef?" Instead it's, "Where's the cash?" You are not interested in <u>Who Moved My Cheese</u>, you want to know who ate my greenbacks. With the catering action and continued strong sales in the Low-Cal Pizza part of the business you should have more money to work with than you do. What is wrong with this picture?

Upon meeting with your accountant you express your dismay. After listening closely to your story the accountant makes a suggestion. "Perhaps you should do what is called an **activity-based costing study,**" he suggests. "I will give you a quick lesson in how to go about doing it, or I will do it for you. It will be far less expensive it you do it yourself, and it really isn't difficult." You opt for the do-it-yourself mode, and after some tutoring as to how to do such a study, you leave the accountant's office and head back to your home turf.

After a reasonable amount of paper shuffling, you locate the document with which you did your original computations. With the coaching you received from your accountant, you immediately see that the only factor driving your decision was the contribution margin, the same factor you were concentrating on as you drove back to your office.

The accountant did not "bad mouth" contribution margin or play down its importance. As a matter of fact he said the C/M figure is critical to almost every decision you make. He went on, however, to remind you that some business transactions require more resources than others. The idea of an activity-based cost analysis is to include ALL of the pertinent information in the decision-making process. When you were learning about RELEVANT COSTING, you were encouraged to eliminate factors that were of no consequence. That practice does not give one a license to take a meat-axe and chop off everything but the C/M factors.

Now that you understand this, you give some consideration to the other costs that have arisen as a result of your entering the catering business. It doesn't take you very long to identify those cost items and you lay them out on the lower portion of the original work-paper.

Exhibit 4

CATERING PRICING SCHEDULE

	PIZZA	DINNER
VARIABLE COSTS	$ 1.08	$ 1.50
DESIRED CONTRIBUTION	$ 1.75	$ 1.25
PRICE PER PERSON SERVED	$ 2.83	$ 2.75

CATERING INCREMENTAL COSTS

DELIVERY VEHICLE COSTS	$ 800.00	
ORDER TAKING & SCHEDULING	$ 300.00	
DELIVERY EMPLOYEE COSTS	$1,000.00	
ORDER PREPARATION COSTS	$ 300.00	
TOTAL INCREMENTAL COSTS		$2,400.00
AVG. NUMBER SERVED MONTHLY		$1,200.00
INCREMENTAL COST PER PERSON		$ 2.00

REVISED CATERING PRICING SCHEDULE

	PIZZA	DINNER
VARIABLE COSTS	$1.08	$1.50
INCREMENTAL COSTS	$2.00	$2.00
CONTRIBUTION MARGIN	$1.75	$1.25
(PRICE ROUNDING)	$0.02	$0.00
REVISED PRICE	$4.85	$4.75

A review of Exhibit #4 reveals what the pricing for catering services should be if you hope to produce the same contribution to the bottom- line. Your original pricing strategy is at least two dollars low per person served. Now do you know who ate the greenbacks? It was your customers because you seem to have added those $2.00 gifts to the menu as no-charge dessert items.

You lean back in your chair, deep in thought as you gaze at the numbers. In a short while you utter, barely loud enough to be heard, the following: "How could I be so #@%#@ (here you may fill in your own choice of words) stupid?"

That is an appropriate question, but not quite on the mark. The question more correctly is, "How could I act in such a stupid manner or make such a stupid decision?" It isn't the intellect of the decision-maker that should be brought into question. The manner by which the decision was made is the culprit. And by the way, don't start patting yourself on the back for making a top-of-the line bad decision; doing so is really quite easy. If you would like the recipe for raising your skill level at using poor judgment and making sub-standard decisions, here it is:

1. Act hastily; you are a hot shot and don't have time to think things through.

2. Don't wait to get all of the facts that you can; with your level of expertise that isn't necessary.

3. If you happen to find yourself in a situation where all of the pertinent facts are at hand, ignore the ones that do not support your original thinking. Never let facts interfere or contradict your "gut feelings." Your ideas are generally the greatest things since sliced bread.

On the slim chance that you might actually be interested in improving your decision-making skills, you might want to try reversing the above steps: Take your time, get all of the facts that you can, and consider all of the facts, whether or not you like what you see. Taking action immediately, without giving the problem sufficient thought, may in some instances be beneficial, but in most situations, such behavior will likely prove to have been a mistake.

Once there were two bulls, one young and "gung ho" and the second one older and wiser, standing on a hill overlooking the dale below. The younger of the two looked down and remarked to his senior partner, "Wow, look at all those cows, let's run down and get ONE." The more experienced bovine replied, "Take it easy son, let's walk down and get them ALL."

The new pricing may cost you some business, but so what? Keeping customers at the old price was costing, not earning you money. If the quality of your products and service are superior, you will do just fine.

The message here should be clear. Rather than focusing on just the contribution margin, you must look at ALL of the cost incurred in providing a product or service. As you were shown in the preceding example, there is more to pricing a product or service than just the spread between direct costs and billing price. Although contribution margin is a very important number, is it not the only figure upon which one must concentrate.

Are we talking rationale thinking here? Absolutely! Unfortunately, because cost/volume/profit analysis and the concept of contribution margin are such powerful tools, it's easy to become trapped by a pattern of thinking that is too narrow in scope.

Donald R. Dignam, MBA, CPA

KEY CONCEPT

You must win the battles before you can win the war.

"Rome was not built in a day."

Chapter 10

Rigidity Versus Flexibility

A reminder: VARIABLE COSTS change <u>in total</u> with the volume of activity, while FIXED COSTS remain constant <u>in total</u> despite changes in the level of activity, within what we earlier defined as the RELEVANT RANGE. All companies have some combination of fixed and variable costs; that combination is known as a COST STRUCTURE.

An organization's cost structure has a dramatic effect upon its contribution-margin ratio (contribution-margin dollars / sales dollars). Here is an illustration:

	COMPANY A	COMPANY B
Total sales	$200,000	$200,000
Variable costs	125,000	75,000
Contribution margin	$ 75,000	$125,000
Fixed costs	50,000	100,000
Net income	$ 25,000	$ 25,000
Contribution-margin ratios	.375	.625

We will recast the above statements assuming that each company experiences a ten percent increase in sales activity.

	COMPANY A	COMPANY B
Total sales	$220,000	$220,000
Variable costs	137,500	82,500
Contribution margin	$ 82,500	$137,500
Fixed costs	50,000	100,000

Net Income	$ 32,500	$ 37,500
Contribution-margin ratios	.375	.625

Note that with the same increase in sales-dollars Company B's profit grew by $12,500 while the profit of Company A was enhanced by only $7,500.

Clearly, in times of increasing sales, it is advantageous to have a cost-structure that tends toward a larger fixed-cost component. Does it work the same way in times of declining sales volume? Let's see:

	COMPANY A	COMPANY B
Total sales	$180,000	$180,000
Variable costs	112,500	67,500
Contribution margin		$ 67,500 $
112,500		
Fixed costs	50,000	100,000
Net income	$ 17,500	$ 12,500
Contribution-margin ratios	.375	.625

In this period of declining sales the opposite swing in profitability took place.

Managers must be aware of the impact that changes in an organization's cost structure can have on its profitability. A larger variable cost component provides management with greater flexibility, but at the price of smaller increases in profits in times of increasing sales-volume. On the other hand, having a large fixed cost component can be a real advantage as sales increase, but can be very painful during slowdowns in business activity. So what is a manager to do?

We suggest heeding the old adage, "Look before you leap." Make, to the best of your ability, and using all available resources, an assessment of what the sales-future of your product might be. Where is your product in its life cycle? Are you first into the market with few competitors, or are other firms beginning to enter the market with clones of what you are selling? Is some new technology just over the horizon that will have a negative impact on your product? If you decide to shift toward more fixed costs via equipment additions, will you actually eliminate any of the existing variable costs? Are there alternative uses to which the new fixed cost item can be put, if demand for the current product utilization diminishes? It is common sense that the greater the fixed cost component of the cost structure, the less flexibility the manager has at his or her disposal.

Leaning in the variable cost direction affords the manager with greater flexibility. If sales activity declines because of a general recession or because of inroads being made by competitors, adjustments can be made fairly quickly. If need be, personnel can be laid off, for example. Of course this strategy weakens the advantage of having a high level of contribution margin.

Unfortunately, there are no canned answers that are the correct ones in any given situation. Once again, management skills must be employed in an attempt to make the best decision possible in the circumstances. Management involves planning, directing, and controlling, all of which entail decision-making. The management toolbox—don't leave home without it.

There are few other things one needs to take into consideration when wrestling with the FIXED/variable versus the fixed/VARIABLE mix question.

The first of these is a concept known as the **margin of safety**. Earlier in your reading, you were introduced to the concept of the breakeven point, the point in sales at which all fixed costs were covered. Beyond that point, profits begin to emerge, and before the breakeven point, losses are being incurred. The arithmetic difference between total sales and the breakeven-point sales is the margin of safety. For Example:

Total Sales	$300,000
Breakeven Sales	225,000
Margin of Safety	$ 75,000

In this example the numbers tell management that total sales can decline by as much as $75,000 before losses will begin to accumulate. Let's see how that works:

Total Sales	$300,000	$225,000
Variable Costs	266,700	200,000
Contribution Margin	$ 33,700	$ 25,000
Fixed Costs	25,000	25,000
Net Income	$ 8,300	Breakeven

The margin of safety can also be expressed as a percentage. In this case, the percentage is twenty-five: $75,000 / $300,000 = .25; That is a reasonable number, because sales volume can decline by as much as one-fourth before the red ink begins to show up.

In the above example, we see a very high ratio of variable costs ($200,000) to fixed cost ($25,000), a ratio of eight to one. Assume that you make a number of management decisions that change the cost structure so that the ratio of fixed–to-variable costs drops to four to one. What follows is the new picture:

Total Sales	$300,000	$225,000
Variable Costs	240,000	180,000
Contribution Margin	$ 60,000	$ 45,000
Fixed Costs	45,000	45,000
Net Income	$ 15,000	$Breakeven

Profits have almost doubled, and the reason is that the contribution margin ratio has increased from 11.1 percent to 15 percent. Once again we emphasize the importance of contribution margin, and that underscores the importance of being able to define costs as being either fixed or variable. If you do not have a sound grasp of how various cost elements will behave in the future, you will have a very difficult time making correct decisions.

There remains one other item we want you to consider before we leave this topic, and that is a concept called **Operating Leverage**. When we use the term "leverage" we are talking about an arrangement or tool that permits us to gain a multiple of output from a given input. If I leverage borrowing to earn more from investing (Arbitraging), I am using leverage. Simply stated, borrow against a whole-life insurance policy at five percent and invest the money at eight percent. Or, issue bonds at eight percent and generate profits in my business of 15 percent.

Operating leverage works like this. First we calculate our **degree of leverage** by dividing total contribution margin by net income. In the preceding example we had net income of $15,000 and contribution margin of $60,000. A division of those numbers results in a degree of leverage of four ($60,000 / $15,000). For each one-percentage point increase in sales, with an operating leverage of four, we should see an increase in profits of four percent. Let's look at the numbers.

	BASE DATA	REVISED DATA
Total Sales	$300,000	$360,000
Variable Costs	240,000	288,000
Contribution Margin	$ 60,000	$ 72,000
Fixed Costs	45,000	45,000
Net Income	$ 15,000	$ 27,000

The profit increased by $12,000; that is an 80 percent increase, and that is four times the 20 percent increase in sales volume. Obviously, we want to strive for a high degree of operating leverage and that typically will result from having a cost structure that is shifted toward higher fixed costs.

In a previous example, we saw two firms that had almost the opposite mix of fixed and variable costs. One had a contribution margin ratio of .375 and the other had a ratio of .625 while both earned the same net income. The firm with the ratio of .625 has a degree of operating leverage of nine while the other firm's degree of leverage was 3.858. Clearly the ratio of nine is the more desirable of the two, but remember, if sales are going down rather than up, the picture is going to be quite different.

KEY CONCEPT

Know your cost structure and the ramifications of making changes to it.

Get it right,

Ready, Fire, Aim is not the correct sequence; It must be Ready, Aim, Fire.

Anonimous

Chapter 11

Beware Of The "Allocators,"
Or Is That Alligators?

All business organizations have two groups of units that either produce income and consume resources via their activities, or simply consume resources. Those that generate income are typically called profit **centers**, and those that do not are called **cost centers**. Let's look at a general merchandise store where one might go to purchase shoes, wearing apparel, small household appliances, bird seed, etc. All of these store areas, or departments, are generating revenues by selling products to customers. These are the revenue or profit centers.

In addition, if we looked closely, we would see some people doing paperwork, like paying bills from vendors or preparing paychecks for employees. We would also come across a shipping and receiving department, an administrative office, perhaps an employee dressing/rest-period room, and a security office. None of these areas has the wherewithal to produce income, yet they still consume resources- these are cost centers. If an organization is to succeed, financially, it must recover all of its cost plus something extra that is referred to as a profit. The entity must not only recover the cost of resources consumed in the revenue centers, wages to sales people for example; the entity must also recoup the cost of the resources consumed in the various cost centers.

Frequently this cost recovery is accomplished by setting prices high enough in the revenue centers to generate an amount of dollars that is adequate to cover all cost incurred and produce a profit. The cost originating in the cost centers is often referred to as **overhead**.

PERFORMANCE REPORT BY DEPARTMENT

October 2002

	Shoes	**Pet Supplies**	**Apparel**
Sales	$50,000	$20,000	$50,000
Variable Costs	25,000	10,000	25,000
Contribution Margin	$25,000	$10,000	$25,000
Overhead Costs	10,000	15,000	20,000
Profit (Loss)	$15,000	($ 5,000)	$ 5,000

All three of these departments had a contribution margin ratio of fifty-percent, yet one appears to have a twenty-five percent loss on sales, one has an apparent thirty percent profit on sales, and the third seems to have a profit of ten percent of sales even though it generated the same total contribution margin as another department with the same sales-volume.

It does not take a lot of searching to locate the answer with regard to why the profit discrepancies appear in the above data; the overhead that has been assigned to these departments is the "culprit."

Assignment of overhead, also known as **overhead allocation**, is an accounting method of transferring the expenses of the COST CENTERS to the REVENUE CENTERS, and it is done because, as mentioned above, the cost centers have no means of directly recovering their costs. Even if these allocations are done in some rational manner, they still involve estimates and assumptions.

Assume the building being occupied contains 100,000 square feet of space, and that it takes $12,000 to heat and maintain the building. Assume further that the revenue centers occupy 80,000 square feet, and the remaining 20,000 square feet are used by activities in the cost centers. An assumption is made that there is a direct relationship between the amount of space and the consumption of resources used to heat and maintain the building. Because the objective of the allocation is to end up with ALL COSTS in the revenue centers, the figure of 80,000 square feet is used rather than the full 100,000 square feet contained in the building.

Therefore: $12,000 of cost / 80,000 Sq. Ft. = $0.15 per Sq. Ft.

After a determination is made with regard to the number of square feet occupied by each department, the following overhead allocations are made.

Shoe Department   10,000 Sq. Ft X $0.15 = $ 1,500
Pet Supplies   4,000 Sq. Ft X $0.15 = $ 600
Apparel Department   15,000 Sq. Ft. X $0.15 = $2,250

The remainder of the expense for heat and maintenance would be assigned to the other revenue centers in the same manner. In this instance, the **cost driver** is believed to be the number of square feet being used by the revenue center.

An effort must be made to find a meaningful cost driver for the distribution of costs from each of the cost centers. Payroll services and human resource services might be allocated using the number of employees in the revenue centers as the cost driver. Shipping and receiving cost might be distributed on the basis of sales-dollars using the assumption that the more merchandise a department sells, the more shipping and receiving resources it will cause to be consumed.

Cost should be allocated only when they cannot be traced with reasonable accuracy in a cost effective manner to a specific activity. Directly assigning costs, when possible, is far superior to allocating costs, because direct assignment is less arbitrary and does not require making assumptions.

Moreover, the inclusion of allocated costs in decision-making data can, at times, confuse the person evaluating the data and thereby lead to poor decision-making. Here is an example of how that might happen:

October 2002

	Shoes	**Pet Supplies**	**Apparel**
Sales	$50,000	$20,000	$50,000
Variable Costs	25,000	10,000	25,000
Contribution Margin	$25,000	$10,000	$25,000
Overhead Costs	10,000	15,000	20,000
Profit (Loss)	$15,000	($ 5,000)	$ 5,000

Net Profit for the combined departments: $15,000

Based upon the information contained in the above report it would appear that closing the Pet Supplies Department might make sense. BE CAREFUL!

Watch out for the "Alligators;" those allocated costs that eat up contribution margin. What follows is a report with more details regarding the allocated overhead.

	Shoes	**Pet Supplies**	**Apparel**
Sales	$50,000	$20,000	$50,000
Variable Costs	25,000	10,000	25,000
Contribution Margin	$25,000	$10,000	$25,000
Overhead Costs:			
Heat	2,000	3,000	4,000
Building Rent	3,000	4,000	6,000
Building Insurance	500	1,300	1,200
Maintenance	3,500	3,200	4,000

Administration	<u>1,000</u>	<u>3,500</u>	<u>4,800</u>
Net Income	$15,000	($5,000)	$ 5,000

In all likelihood, the majority of the overhead allocated to the Pet Supplies Department is not avoidable costs. That means the total cost of these items will remain the same whether or not the department is closed. If that is the case, the department's previously allocated share of the overhead will simply be shifted to the remaining departments. Here is what happens to your department's performance report if the "suits" decide to eliminate the Pet Supplies Department:

	Shoe Department	Apparel Department
Previous Net Income	$15,000	$ 5,000
Added O/H Allocation	<u>7,500</u>	<u>7,500</u>
Revised Net Income	$ 7,500	($ 2,500)

Number one, if your bonus is dependent upon the performance of your department, as it likely is, you will take a beating for a decision someone else made because you were burdened with cost over which you had no control.

Number two, the company is worse off, because it gave up $10,000 in contribution margin by closing the Pet Supplies Department but did not reduce overhead costs, because those costs were not avoidable. That is, the company sacrificed $10,000 in potential profit while at the same time it did nothing to reduce fixed costs.

KEY CONCEPT

We echo a previous key concept:don't be mislead by allocated fixed-cost data.

Donald R. Dignam, MBA, CPA

"No man is an island unto himself"
somewhere in the shadows there lurks an allocator.

John Donne

Chapter 12

Variable-Costing Reports

Managers can be helped in understanding what is going on in their businesses financially, and thereby be put into a position to make sound decisions, if the reports they are receiving are restructured. Reports that highlight results that are volume-driven and that aggregate and stress the total fixed-cost burden faced by the organization can enable managers to focus on critical information. Reports of this sort are prepared using a system called **variable costing**.

Financial reports that are prepared in the traditional way array costs and expenses by FUNCTION. That is, sales commissions show up as selling expenses while rent shows up as an administrative expense. Depreciation of the factory building appears as a manufacturing cost, and therefore, part of the cost of goods sold, while the cost of fuel for delivery trucks appears in the report as a part of the operational overhead. As a result of this practice, the overhead expenses are spread throughout the report, and that makes it difficult to get a handle on what the total monthly overhead burden is. At the same time, profits originating from sales activities become contaminated with income results from production activities when quantities produced do not match up with quantities sold.

These problems are addressed, to some degree, by restructuring the financial reports into what are known as VARIABLE COSTING reports. Rather than listing costs/expenses by function, those items are segregated into groups based upon the manner in which they behave. That is,

67

fixed costs are aggregated in one place, while variable costs are summed in another group. The sales commissions mentioned above would be included in the "variable group" because they would vary based upon sales volume, while depreciation of the building would appear in the "fixed group" because the charge for that expense item would be the same, regardless of the sales volume. What follows is a comparison of two types of financial reports: Traditional and Variable:

	Product A	Product B
	Traditional	Variable
Gross Sales	$120,000	$120,000
Returns & Allowances	5,000	5,000
Net Sales	$115,000	$115,000
Variable Cost of Sales	40,000	40,000
Fixed Manufacturing Overhead	10,000	00,000
Gross Profit	$ 65,000	$ 75,000
Variable Selling Expense		15,000
Variable Administrative Expense		12,000
Contribution Margin	$ 65,000	$ 48,000
Variable Selling Expense	15,000	
Variable Administrative Expense	12,000	
Fixed Selling Expense	10,000	10,000
Fixed Administrative Expense	12,000	12,000
Fixed Manufacturing Overhead	- 0 -	10,000
Net Income	$ 16,000	$ 16,000

Note that the net income figure in both of these reports is $16,000. That should always be the case when the total of units sold happens to agree with the total of units produced. When production volume and sales volume differ, the net income figure will also be different. To begin this explanation, we will review unit-cost data for two different levels of production.

	Traditional		**Variable**	
Production Volumes	10,000	20,000	10,000	20,000
Total Costs:				
Variable Manufacturing	$10,000	$20,000	$10,000	$20,000
Fixed Manufacturing	$20,000			
Unit Costs				
Variable Manufacturing	$1.00	$1.00	$1.00	$1.00
Fixed Manufacturing	$2.00	$1.00	$0.00	$0.00
Total Per Unit	$3.00	$2.00	$1.00	$1.00

Note that the per-unit cost fluctuates. If that is true it makes it quite difficult to make predictions about future cost behavior. Is fixed manufacturing cost fixed, or isn't it?

Sales Volume Per @ $50 Per Unit:

	TRADITIONAL		**VARIABLE**	
	10,000	10,000	10,000	10,000
Total Sales	$50,000	$50,000	$50,000	$50,000
Cost of Sales	30,000	20,000	10,000	10,000
Contribution Margin	$ 20,000	$ 30,000	$40,000	$ 40,000
Administrative Overhead	10,000	10,000	10,000	10,000
Manufacturing Overhead	—0—	—0—	10,000	10,000
Net Income	$10,000	$20,000	$20,000	$20,000

Note that even though the sales volume was the same in all four of the above instances, net income doubled under the traditional system of financial reporting. Using the variable reporting system, the profit is constant, the same way that the sales volume is constant, and that makes sense. What is going on here?

The use of the traditional reporting method results in some of the FIXED COSTS being transferred to the balance sheet in the form of increased inventory values, because some of the fixed costs have been included in the manufacturing cost per unit, and the cost of sales is reduced by that same amount. Per-unit inventory prices are $2.00 with traditional reporting, and only $1.00 using variable costing. Therefore, 10,000 units in the inventory at an added one dollar per unit results in the $10,000 difference in the reported net incomes. The added $10,000 is sometimes referred to as "ghost" or "phantom" profits, because eventually the inventoried fixed cost will have to show up in the income statement and lower the reported profit in the period in which that takes place. That situation will arise in any period where sales volumes exceed production volumes.

As soon as a period occurs where sales outstrip production, the higher-priced units will move from inventory to cost of sales. When using traditional costing of inventories it appears that profits are being driven by PRODUCTION rather than by SALES. It is my understanding that sales revenue is the thing that generates profits, while production consumes resources.

KEY CONCEPT

Key Concept

The Measurement of Actual Contribution Margin Can Be Better Gauged By Matching Revenue, a Variable Factor, With Variable Cost

"My wife asked me for a fur coat, so I mated a mink with an orangutan. It was a beautiful coat, but the sleeves were too long."
Henny Youngman

Chapter 13

Standards & Variances From Them?

Way, way back in the beginning, we discussed the need for having some reference point when making decisions regarding cost data. The question of whether some cost element was fixed or variable depended upon our comparing that element's behavior to some benchmark, and we learned that the standard benchmark was generally units of production. When evaluating performance, we also need some yardstick against which the performance can be measured, in order to reach a conclusion as to whether the performance is great, good, fair, or lousy.

I played golf the other day with three others and I shot 95. The scores of the others were 98, 110 and 115. Was my score a good score? Well that depends upon what comparison is being made. If the comparison is based upon the four scores in our group, the answer is probably yes, because it was the best of the four scores. On the other hand, if my score of 95 were compared with what Tiger Woods might have shot on the same course, the answer would most assuredly be lousy.

If your business produced 10,000 pizzas last month at total costs amounting to $20,000, is that the good, the bad or the ugly? Who cares? You should, if your profits and continued operation depend upon the answer to that question.

Management accountants have developed a tool to help provide an answer to the questions of was it good or bad, and if so, how good or how bad. The tool is called **standard cost**

accounting, or **standard costing**. Standards are targets to which performances can be compared.

Standards come in a variety of flavors, among which are ideal standards and practical standards. Ideal standards presume that absolutely nothing will go wrong in a process and that every minute of time is productive time. The game of golf was mentioned earlier. A normal round of golf includes eighteen holes; at each of them, the player drives a ball from the tee. An ideal standard would be a score of 18, eighteen holes with one stroke on each hole. I once played golf with a gorilla that could drive the ball a mile. For that player, a score of eighteen might have been a reasonable standard; it could hit the green from every tee. Unfortunately, it putted the same way it drove the ball, a mile. Therefore, unless one happens to be playing miniature golf, an ideal standard is unrealistic, and attempting to achieve it will almost certainly result in disappointments and frustration.

A practical standard, on the other hand, is one that is achievable if most things go as planned. In golf, that standard is called par. Practical standards are not only "doable," they can, on occasion, be surpassed. Practical standards are the ones against which performances should be measured.

The measurement of performance against a standard will result in a finding that the performance was below, equal to, or greater than the standard. Performances that are below or above the standard result in what managers refer to as **variances**. Variances that are better than the standard are looked upon as being favorable, and those that are below standard are considered unfavorable. Managers need to investigate these variances, because by doing so they may learn ways to improve the process under study.

The analysis of deviations from some standard leads us back to the need for managers and their good judgment. Almost invariably, each analysis will result in some variance. In one case, it might be learned that the standard was missed by one-tenth of one percent, and in another, the discrepancy might be ten percent. Management's time is a limited resource. Where should that limited resource be employed? Chasing the one-tenth of one percent variation, or the ten percent difference from the "norm?" Computers can spit out the variances, but it is up to human beings to decide which ones are worthy of further study. If you are really managing, a computer will not replace you, but if you act like a robot, you may very well find yourself in search of a new business opportunity.

The process of analyzing deviations from standards is called **variance analysis**. (Isn't that clever?) Being aware of the fact that a variance has occurred isn't, in and of itself, terribly helpful. One needs to know what caused the variance, before one can take corrective action. This relates back to an earlier chapter; the diagnosis must be made before the course of therapy is prescribed. If, in shooting my golf score of 95, I hit every green in regulation and then three-putted every green, it should be fairly obvious that time spent on the putting green is likely to be more helpful than going to the driving range. Let's take a quick look at making a diagnosis.

Let us return to your pizza business that, through your application of sound management accounting tools, has grown to ten locations.

Because of the economy of scale it provides, you have gone to centralized-purchasing of the ingredients needed to make pizzas. Moreover, through the experience you have gained, you have determined that 100 pounds of ingredients with a total cost of $200 should produce 50 medium-sized pizzas; in other words, you have developed what accountants call **material standards**.

A review of a monthly report from one of your locations indicates that in using 160 pounds of supplies at a total cost of $300, only 70 pizzas were produced. Based upon the material standard you developed, 160 pounds of ingredients should have produced 80 pizzas. Therefore, you have discovered a variance that is worth investigating.

What should have taken place: 160 lbs/2 Lbs Each   = 80 Pizzas
What did happen: 160 Lbs/2.29 Lbs Each =70 Pizzas

This situation needs to be investigated because the yield of final product from 160 pounds of ingredients is only 87.5 percent of what it should be. Moreover, the dollar-cost per finished pizza is 14.5 percent higher than it should be. There are at least two reasons why these discrepancies exist: Too much paid for a pound of ingredients, or excessive use of ingredients. It could also be a mix of both of those reasons. Here again, we need to take out the stethoscope to help us diagnose the cause of the problem before we can search for a cure.

First we will look at the quantity of ingredients used issue:

Actual Output = 70 Pizzas @ 2 lbs. Per Pizza   = 140 Lbs.
Actual Output = 70 Pizzas @ 2.29 lbs. Per Pizza = 160 Lbs.
Unfavorable Utilization   (20 Lbs.)
Standard Price Per Pound   X $2.00
   USAGE VARIANCE (Unfavorable)   ($40.00)
The first line above is the standard.

Next we will investigate the price issue:

Actual Purchases = 160 Lbs @ 2.00 Per Lb.   = $320.00

Actual Purchases = 160 Lbs @ 1.875 Per Lb.　=　 300.00
Purchase Price Variance – Favorable　　　**$ 20.00**

It seems that in place of answering the question, "Why did the variance occur?" we have raised two more questions. Well, we have, and that is what managing your business, or your department, or your life is all about; continuing to ask and answer questions, until you get to the root of the problem you perceive to exist.

You now need to discuss the apparent over-utilization of ingredients with the manager of the location where the variance came to pass. Was it the result of being provided with inferior ingredients, because of the low price paid for them, or was it just sloppy work on the part of the employees who make the pizzas? If the answer is sloppy work, the manager of that location needs to get his act together, and you must congratulate the purchasing-person for a job well done. On the other hand, if the less-than-desired results arose because of inferior ingredients, you need to counsel the purchasing-person regarding the need to maintain quality standards.

We need to point out something you may have not noticed. When we were studying the cost of ingredients, or price variance, we used the quantity of ingredients PURCHASED, because the act of purchasing is what drives the cost of acquisition.

When we were looking at the variance for the amount of ingredients used issue, we used just that, the amount USED, not the amount purchased. It is the quantity actually used that drives the quantity variance.

This separation is necessary because the price variance will be discussed with personnel in the Purchasing Department, while the quantity questions are being directed to production personnel.

This type of analysis can also be used in looking at the other factors involved in generating the cost of a product or service. In the previous paragraphs, we looked at the effect using lower-priced ingredients at higher volumes had on the final cost of production. Why did neither of those two things, price or quantity consumed, lead us to the answer we needed to really be effective in remedying the problem?

Is it perhaps a labor-efficiency situation? The same technique is used in these analyses as was used when dealing with the ingredients-cost question, and as was the case then, two possible causes for the variance from the standard exist: labor-rates were too high, or too many hours were consumed in accomplishing the tasks. But which of those two possibilities is it?

First, we will look at the question of wage rates. Your market area suggests that pizza makers earn $6.00 per hour, and so you set that figure as your standard.

A review of the payroll for the period in which the 70 pizzas were produced indicates that employees were paid for 20 hours of work at a total cost of $101.50. That indicates an hourly rate of $5.80.

When trying to learn the effect of one factor, that factor must be isolated so that it is what is driving, or causing, the difference in the final numbers; it is the dependent variable. If you decide to change to a new brand of golf balls with the hope of increasing your driving distance, you need to set up a test that will let you make a reasonable judgment about the effect of the new brand of balls. You must try to hold all of the other factors constant. Therefore, you must use the same set of clubs, play the same course, under the same weather conditions, and perhaps play with the same three other people in your foursome. Now if your driving improves or deteriorates, there is some basis to assume that the new brand of balls is the cause. (Unless you are a member of the PGA, however, I would not bet the house on it.)

In looking at the wage-rate effect we will do the same thing; we will keep the other factor, time, constant.

Actual Hours of 20 X $5.80 = $116.00
Actual Hours of 20 X $6.00 = $120.00

This measurement, where we held the **quantity of hours constant** indicates that we saved some money via the lower wage rate. That is good news, and the management-accounting jargon for it is **labor rate variance**.

Now we will take a look at something called the **labor efficiency variance**. Here we will hold the wage-rate constant and concentrate on the quantity of labor-hours consumed. The first step is to make a decision regarding the number it should have taken to produce 70 pizzas. Having spent a lot of time sweating in the kitchen when you first began your business, you know that a decent pizza-maker should to be able to turn out four pizzas per hour, one every fifteen minutes, even taking into account breaks and order wait-time. Given that, we see the following:

70 pizzas @ ¼ hours each is   17.5 hours
Total Actual Hours Paid This Period Was 20.0 hours

It appears that an extra 2.5 hours of payroll cost crept into the system so here we go again:

Actual Hours Paid 20.0 X $6.00   = $120.00

Standard Hours Required 17.5 X $6.00 = $105.00

This computation indicates that an extra $15.00 in wages cost was the result of inefficient productivity by the persons who create the pizzas.

The net of the two computations is that $4.00 was saved by paying a lower wage rate, but, perhaps because of employing less skilled pizza makers, an additional expenditure for an extra 2.5 hours of productive time was required. The bottom line is that a $4.00 labor-rate savings, and a $15.00 labor efficiency variance suggest that paying higher wages for more skilled employees may make sense. (Ever hear the expression, "you get what you pay for.")

Operating a business or managing a department is not easy; it takes hard work if one wishes to be successful. And a part of that work is asking the correct questions and keep digging until you find the correct answers.

KEY CONCEPT

**Don't stop when you learn the answer to "What?";
keep at it until you have learned the answer to "Why?"**

As one of the patriots at the time of the American revolution is reported to have said, "...As for me, give me a reason for why the numbers read as they do, or give me death!"
Patrick Henry

79

Chapter 14

Things Don't Just Happen,
S—Happens If One Does Not Plan

During the course of the preceding pages, especially in the case of the pizza business, new ideas for improving profitability kept popping up. Those ideas all seemed to fit with some general course of action aimed at growing the business and the size of its bottom line. Actions of that sort usually arise when one is "playing it by ear." Playing it by ear would seem to imply that something has happened that has caused a sound. If one is reacting to a sound, then one must be reacting to something in the past.

If one happens to be a cosmologist reacting to what has taken place in the past, makes sense, because cosmologists are, in fact, looking back in time. However, those scientists are not looking back in time with an aim toward changing anything, because they understand the fact that, as far as we know today, one cannot change the past. Cosmologists are trying to learn what happened many, many, many years ago, and why.

Managers, as pointed out at the very beginning of this book, must be focused upon the future. Just as one cannot change the past, one cannot control what happens in the future with absolute certainty. Having a plan of action and a goal in mind can, in many instances, reduce the level of uncertainty considerably.

I have a client whose business is making little headway toward the owner's goals. The reason for that is the absence of a well-developed plan of action for the future. Every few months, this owner comes up with a new idea and begins to drive the business in a new direction. This sort of behavior is akin to trying to reach the goal of driving to California from New York in the absence of a road map or a time schedule.

Assuming you will do the manly-thing of not stopping to ask for directions, it is likely that it will cost you a considerable amount of time and money, before you reach your destination, if you ever do get there. You may begin driving west for a while, then turn south, then back west again. Occasionally, you will see something of interest along the way and stop to take a look. These side trips will hinder your progress, of course. One may find it difficult to find fault with your goal, but shooting holes in your methodology is a piece of cake, and your "friends" just love to shoot down your behavior.

The client referred to above is currently in the process of negotiating with his banker to increase his loan balance. A foundation for a new building is in the ground, and NOW he is trying to borrow money to put a building on the foundation. Better planning might have avoided the stress of this situation, not to mention arriving at better terms for the loan.

When you are operating a business, you are the driver; it is you who must decide where the company is going, what route it is going to follow, and when it will reach its destination. DO NOT just get in and turn the key in the ignition, if you are serious about getting somewhere that is worth the trip. We are talking about profit planning here; something that was, and in some circles still is referred to as budgeting. (Budgeting is not a swear word.)

There is more than one type of business plan: Strategic plans, operation plans, cash-flow plans, and capital-expenditure plans. The development of these plans usually follows in the sequence of the plans listed above.

Strategic planning deals with what type of company we are; what business we are in; who are our competitors; what the weaknesses of our competitors are; how we can exploit those weaknesses; what are our strengths are, and how we can gain maximum advantage from those strengths.

Once these questions have been answered, one can begin to develop the plan of operation. There are two basic approaches that can be adopted. One is the balance sheet or financial position approach. The other is the income statement approach, or net income approach.

Exhibit #4

Budgeting Balance Sheets

ASSETS	December 31, 2003	RESULTS REQUIRED	December 31, 2004
Current Assets			
Cash & Equivalents	$ 100,000	$ 10,000	$ 110,000
Accounts Receivable	$ 250,000	$ (25,000)	$ 225,000
Inventories	$ 200,000	$ (10,000)	$ 190,000
Total Current Assets	$ 550,000		$ 525,000
Plant & Equipment	$ 500,000		$ 500,000
Total Assets	$ 1,050,000	$ (25,000)	$ 1,025,000
Liabilities & Equity			
Current Liabilities			
Accounts Payable	$ 90,000		$ 90,000
Notes Payable	$ 50,000		$ 50,000
Other Current Liabilities	$ 25,000		$ 25,000

Total Current Liabilities	$ 165,000			$ 165,000
Long-Term Debt	$ 350,000	$ (87,500)		$ 262,500
Equity	$ 535,000	$ 62,500		$ 597,500
Total Liabs. & Equity	$ 1,050,000	$ (25,000)		$ 1,025,000

Exhibit #4 shows the results of the first step taken when using the balance sheet approach. The two left columns of numbers depict the organization's financial picture at the beginning of the planning year. The two columns furthest to the right represent the target balance sheet at the close of the year for which the plan will be developed. The center column describes the changes that senior management wants to see take place over the course of the year.

The desired changes are:
Increase the ending cash balance by: $ 10,000
Decrease Accounts Receivable balances by: $ 25,000
Reduce Inventories by: $ 10,000
Decrease Long-Term Debt by: $ 87,500
Increase Equity by: $ 62,500

This information will now be communicated with the executives and managers of the various segments of the business, so that detailed operating plans can be formulated. Those plans will culminate in a budgeted income statement and a cash budget, which will provide the road map by which the targeted balance sheet will be reached.

The budgeted-income statement will exactly resemble the income statements that are prepared regularly and begin, of course, with the budgeted sales. The sales budget is the first step in developing the operating plan, because all other budgetary planning is a function of the anticipated sales.

Planning production and administrative support budgets in the absence of a reasonably accurate sales budget is a total waste of time. Moreover, without knowing the sales budget, the source of cash receipts, or the other budgets, the cause of expenditures, it is impossible to develop a cash-flow budget upon which one can hang his or her hat. Trying to do so will likely end up hanging the person who laid out the cash-management plan.

Exhibit #5

BUDGETED INCOME STATEMENT

<u>FOR THE YEAR ENDING DECEMBER 31, 2004</u>

Net Sales Revenue	$1,100,000	100.00%
Cost of Goods Sold	<u>$655,000</u>	<u>59.50%</u>
Gross Profit	$445,000	40.50%
Selling & Administrative Expense	<u>$382,500</u>	<u>34.80%</u>
Net Operating Income *	$62,500	5.70%

BUDGET STATEMENT OF CASH FLOW

FOR THE YEAR ENDING DECEMBER 31, 2004

Cash Balance @ January 1, 2004		$100,000
Sources of Cash:		
Cash From Operations	$62,500	
Reduction of Accounts Receivable	$25,000	
Reduction of Inventory	$10,000	$97,500
Available Cash		$197,500
Uses of Cash:		
Reduction of Long-Term Debt		-$87,500
Cash Balance @ December 31, 2004		$110,000

* The Cause of The Equity Growth

Exhibit #5 contains a budgeted-income statement and a budget showing expected cash receipts and expenditures for the year. If the plans depicted in these two documents can be made to come to fruition, senior management's balance sheet targets will be reached.

The income statement approach is, of course, the exact reverse. In that instance senior managers would set a target profit for the coming year, and a budgeted income statement would be built through the planning process. After the income budget is constructed, the cash budget will follow, except that this budget would be modified to take into consideration any plans for capital expenditures, debt reduction, and/or future borrowings. As a last step, the budgeted balance sheet will be prepared.

For most businesses, and in one's personal financial planning, the cash budget is critical. It has been widely repeated that most new, small businesses fail because they run out of cash. Obviously, personal bankruptcies, which are on the rise, are clearly the result of running out of cash. Somewhere in scripture, I believe, it is said "Man does not live by bread alone." I am sure the coiner of that statement wasn't talking about credit cards, but who lives without them today?

There is nothing inherently wrong with credit cards; in fact, they can and do serve many useful purposes, such as creating clean, auditable records of expenditures. The problems associated with credit cards don't emerge because people use them. The problems are the result of failing to budget cash flow and live within that budget.

We stated at the outset that Running The Numbers, and being sure that you are looking at the numbers that count, is critical to success. With regard to credit card use, the credit-limit number is not the one to be watching; the cash needed to meet your obligations is the key figure.

KEY CONCEPT

**Planning can be a pain,
but acting before you do so can be even more painful
because
without a plan you don't know where you are going.**

I came home from work one evening to find my wife's car in the dining room. I asked, "How did you that?" and she replied, "It was easy; I just made a left turn when I came out of the kitchen."

Henny Youngman

Chapter 15

Putting It All Together

Let's try to pull most of what has gone before together in one scenario.

The pizza business you began several years ago has been wildly successful, much more so than in your wildest imagination you ever thought it would be. It has been so successful, in fact, that you have recently purchased an NBA franchise, and you are now the not-so-proud owner of the Charleston **Champs**, currently being referred to by fans as the Charleston **Chumps**. The season has just ended, and the final team record stands at 35 wins and 47 losses. The team did not make the playoffs. You are not happy!

The vice-president for basketball operations is not happy either. He is particularly unhappy because he is unemployed, as is the former coach.

Before refilling the management roster you decide you need to make some decisions regarding what is needed to return the Chumps to their previous status as Champs. Once you have a plan of action in place (and remember, planning is an essential tool for reaching goals), you will then seek out persons who are a good fit.

You are not a rocket-scientist. As a matter of fact, you are a pizza guy, but even a pizza guy realizes that the players on the floor, not unlike the cooks in the kitchen, are the ones who make the difference between success and failure, so your first step is to review the existing roster of players.

The first step you take is to array the names of the players, the positions they fill, and their stats for the just-ended disastrous season. In the course of doing that, you think back over the season to the games you could have, should have, might have won. Two clear impressions etch themselves into your gray matter: You don't have a pure out-side shooter, and when your floor leader has to sit out for a rest, the team's play resembles a Chinese fire drill.

You now have in front of you the liabilities, the absence of an out-side shooter and the lack of a back-up floor leader, and the assets, the existing roster. What you have done is begin to employ the **THEORY OF CONSTRAINTS**. Your first bottleneck is the lack of a person who can take charge when your starting floor leader has to take a break or fouls out. Lacking that person, you don't need the pure shooter because it isn't likely that that person will get the ball at the opportune time anyway.

Assuming you can find a way to release that constraint, you can move on to the number two constraint, which is the need for a shooter.

"Piece of cake," let's do it. Hold it, this is the NBA, and there is such a thing as a salary cap. You have almost no room for paying "big bucks" to some established super star. Another constraint!

No problem, just draft the next Michael Jordan with your high draft pick, driven by the team's miserable showing in the just-ended season. (Please, don't remind me.) But wait, what are the odds of drafting a player who will evolve into the next Michael Jordan? I would say slim and none. (**We are back to the risk versus rewards issue.**) How many potential superstars who have signed contracts with outlandish signing bonuses and multi-year contracts have earned their keep?

Okay already, I am doing my best to think this through; this isn't exactly like making pizzas! Ahah! We will go to the free-agent market. Good thinking, but what about the salary-cap constraint?

The obvious answer is to unload some of the existing salaries to free up some room to go shopping. You have in front of you the roster and statistics from the season that just ended. What should you do next? Why not array next to the actual stats the average stats that were used by the players' agents when the existing contracts were negotiated? Sounds like we might be bringing a version of **standard cost accounting and variance analyses** into play here.

That is exactly what you are about to do. You are going to compare actual with expected (the standard) and see what the variances are. Then you are going to focus on the variances, beginning with the largest, and working your way down to the smallest. You must look at both the favorable and unfavorable numbers, because only a few players are untouchable. Those few players who are untouchable are your **irrelevant data**; you can skip wasting time looking at those players' stats. In doing this analysis, you must look for reasons that justify sub-standard performances: Was a player injured, for example.

Next, you write down, or key into your spreadsheet program, the salary cap number to which the league's owners have agreed. From that you must subtract the total of the salaries committed to the "untouchables." You are left with the cash you have to work with in filling the two key positions.

Unless you are the author of a book entitled *Run the Numbers,* cash is always a scare resource, and therefore, a constraint. Here, you should employ what you learned about

maximizing output from a scarce resource. See Exhibit # 6.

Exhibit #6   **EVALUATION OF SCARE RESOURCE UTILIZATION**

	POINTS	BOARDS	ASSISTS	T/OVERS	FOULS	TOTAL
VALUES	6	4	2	-2	-1	
PLAYER						
A	1000	320	720	-60	-320	1660
B	800	160	600	-10	-300	1250
C	1200	480	100	-50	-280	1450
D	900	240	210	-70	-190	1090
E	400	200	200	-40	-60	700
F	300	600	260	-10	-380	700
G	600	210	180	-70	-110	810
TOTALS	5200	2210	2270	-310	-1640	7730

Available Salary-Cap Dollars $7,730,000

Value Per Net Point Produced $1,000

Rank Players By Value Received For Scare Resources:

A	$1,660,000
C	$1,450,000
B	$1,250,000
D	$1,090,000
G	$810,000
F	$770,000
E	$700,000
TOTAL	$7,730,000

The players who are not on the list of untouchables have been listed in alphabetical order with their statistics from the season that just ended. You have assigned values of 6, 4 and 2 points for points scored, rebounds and assists respectively. You have also assigned negative values of two and one for turnovers and fouls. The product of multiplying the point values by the statistics results in a "contribution" per player.

The sum of the contributions divided into the available dollars to stay under the salary cap results in a quotient of $1,000 per net point produced. Multiplication of the contribution points by player by the $1,000 figure, reveals what each player should be earning as his share of available resources.

A comparison of the theoretical contribution value to the actual salaries being paid, leads to a list of those players who will be first to be placed on the trading block.

You are now better prepared to bring in a general manager and a coach, because you have a plan and you know the resources with which you have to work.

Not all of the managerial accounting tools were put to use in dealing with the problem at hand. That is not unusual. Each decision-making situation is unique, and calls for using a different mix of tools and data. If one happens to be power washing one's deck, it is unlikely that a compound miter saw will be of much value.

Early on, it was stated that knowing the numbers that are important in a particular dilemma is important. It is equally important to know what tools need to be brought to bear as you struggle with the decision to be made.

In most instances, punting will not be an option. You will have to break out the playbook and choose the best option, but only after you have accurately **diagnosed the problem.**

Success in business, as in life, doesn't just happen. If one does not get fully involved and fully understand what is going on, s—happens! Through the use of the tools described in this book, it is hoped that you will be able to avoid some of the snafus that can result from being misled by incorrect interpretations of various reports and data analyses. Numeric representations of life's/business situations are of great importance and should not be ignored. Without the ability to express factual situations in numeric terms and equations, we would not be able to explain and understand most of what keeps this world of ours functioning.

On the other side of the coin, however, we find that in the absence of humankind's ability to use its intelligence to interpret, analyze, and utilize the data generated, little progress would be made. An awareness of the fact that the Earth is round is an interesting observation. Knowing that an object in motion will tend to stay in motion in the absence of some resisting force, is also interesting. Putting the two facts together, however, has resulted in humankind's ability to create a space station and put a man on the moon.

The ability to put two and two together, a round earth, and the laws of motion, results in major accomplishments. Those are the LARGE accomplishments, but small steps can make a difference in the long run. Someone once uttered the phrase, "Don't sweat the small stuff, and it is all small stuff." Oh, really? Put a penny in your desk drawer tomorrow morning. The next day, double the contribution: put in two pennies. On the third day put in four pennies, and keep this pattern up for the next thirty days. After all, pennies are certainly "small stuff". If you are able to keep up the doubling-contribution for an entire thirty days you don't need this book. If you are doubtful of that challenge, *Run the Numbers*.

Do not allow yourself to be intimidated by numbers. You need not be a whiz at mathematics to make good use of the data available to you, but you do need to be able to differentiate information from data. Information is power and data is data. Until you are able to put the data into a form that lends insight into some decision-making situation, you don't have any information.

On a cold yet sunny afternoon in February, your spouse comes into the family room and says, "Look dear, I have a list of all of the checks we wrote last year and it totals $30,000. We sure spend a lot of money, and I think we need to reduce it next year, don't you?" You look closely at the person who has just said something about reducing expenditures. You want to make sure that you are in the correct residence, and that this person is actually the one to whom you are married. Having assured yourself that this is not a dream, you readily agree that reducing expenditures is a good idea and ask, "How do you suggest we go about cutting down on our spending?"

Your spouse suggests that reducing spending by ten percent would make a tremendous difference, so why not just go though and decide that we will not write every tenth check? As we spend money next year we will just skip paying whatever item happens to be the tenth one as we pay bills, purchase gifts, etc. Now that is a simple and easily understood approach. Unfortunately, that approach is based upon working with data, rather than working with information.

It might be just as effective to shoot the mailperson each tenth time he/she arrives with bills to put into your mailbox. Effective? Absolutely! Practical? I don't think so. The only effective way to deal with this situation is to convert the data into information and then use tools such as relevant cost, avoidable cost, scarce resource utilization, leverage, etc., to help you make the best choices.

I know that; I wrote *Run the Numbers*. You know that; you have read *Run the Numbers*. All you need to do now is hand him or her a copy of *Run the Numbers* and hope that he or she begins to read before the second half of the game begins. You have plenty of numbers to run already during the second half of the game in order to determine whether or not the various point spreads were covered. At the very least the book has to be read before the mailperson shows up for the tenth time.

I have a dream that one day auditors and clients, sales managers and controllers, production managers and budget directors, IRS agents and taxpayers will all join hands and sing, "Agreement at last, agreement at last, thank God Almighty, we finally agree on the numbers at last."

Dr. Martin Luther King, Jr.

The Lexicon Of

Management Accounting

ABSORPTION COSTING: In this system, the fixed manufacturing overhead does become a part of the unit cost of goods manufactured. This method is acceptable for external reporting purposes. Inventory values will be higher when using absorption costing versus using variable costing.

ACTIVITY-BASED COSTING: A cost-accumulation system, wherein both manufacturing **costs and non-manufacturing costs** are assigned to a product, service, or customer.

AICPA: The American Institute of Certified Public Accountants, which is the national body that represents the accounting profession, publishes *The Journal Of Accounancy,* and prepares the examination that must be completed successfully by persons wishing to become certified public accountants.

AVOIDABLE COST: A future cost that will be altered or eliminated, depending upon what management decisions are made. Avoidable costs are relevant in the decision-making process.

BREAK-EVEN POINT: The volume of sales at which all variable and fixed costs will be recovered via sales revenues.

BREAK-EVEN POINT IN SALES/DOLLARS: The total sales in dollars needed to cover all variable and fixed cost. It can be calculated by dividing the total fixed cost by the gross profit percentage. (Total fixed cost of $1,500 divided by a gross profit of 33% equals a break-even point of $4,545.46 in total sales.)

BREAK-EVEN POINT IN UNITS: The number of products that must be sold to cover all variable and fixed costs. It is calculated by dividing the total fixed cost by the gross profit, in dollars per unit, sold. (Total fixed cost of $1,500 divided by a gross profit of $50 per-unit equal sales of 30 units to break-even.)

CAPITAL BUDGET: Management's plans to acquire property, plant, and equipment.

CMA: Certified Management Accountant, a designation granted by the Institute of Management Accountants once a candidate has passed a qualifying examination and meets and maintains other requirements.

COMMITTED COST: A cost element over which management has little or no control. (When we sign a lease to rent space, we have committed a full year's rent to the cost mix.)

CONTRIBUTION MARGIN: The difference between the selling price of a product/service and the total variable cost, not just the manufacturing costs, of the product/service.

CONTRIBUTION MARGIN RATIO: The percentage derived by dividing the contribution margin, in dollars by the selling price. Quite similar to the gross profit or gross margin calculation.

CONVERSION COST: The combination of direct material and manufacturing overhead costs.

COST: A sub-set of expenses related to the manufacture or purchase of products for resale. It can also be applied to the provision of a service, such as consulting.

COST ACCOUNTING: A sub-set of management that deals primarily with tracking and accumulating the expenses incurred in manufacturing products for sale to others.

COST ALLOCATION: An accounting technique that is used to assign the costs of non-revenue-producing activities to revenue-producing activities and/or to assign manufacturing overhead costs to products. Example: The cost of heating and lighting a building might be "allocated" to revenue-producing departments based upon the number of square feet each department occupies.

COST BEHAVIOR: A term used to describe the potential degree of change, either in total, or on a per-unit basis, in response to changes in the volume of activity in which these costs are consumed. Example: Cheese is an important ingredient in a pizza. The more pizzas that are produced, the more the cost of cheese will increase in total. But, if quality control measures are in place, each pizza of the same size will consume the same amount of cheese, so at the per-unit level the cost of consumption will remain the same.

COST DRIVER: An activity that is presumed to be the cause of resource consumption. Example: Miles driven is a cost driver for the amount of vehicle fuel consumed.

COST STRUCTURE: The combination of fixed and variable costs found in a particular organization as it carries out its purpose. A public utility company would normally have a very high ratio of fixed to variable costs, while a fast-food establishment would have a very high ratio of variable to fixed costs.

COST VARIANCES: The difference between the standard cost and actual incurred cost to produce a product. These variances are generally further sub-divided into price and volume variances.

CPA: "Certified Public Accountant." This is a designation awarded to persons who first qualify for, and then pass an examination dealing with accounting in all of its branches, Federal taxation, attestation (auditing) and commercial law. Many state boards of accountancy require this designation before one may be licensed to practice as a public accountant.

DEGREE OF OPERATING LEVERAGE: An arithmetic computation that assists management in estimating the effect various changes in sales volume will have on operating net income. Example: A contribution margin of $100 and net income of $50 will result in a degree of operating leverage of 2 ($100/$50 =2). Theoretically, for every one percent increase in sales volume the operating net income should increase by two percent.

DIRECT LABOR COSTS: Expenditures for manpower whose efforts can be traced to the production of specific products. (Wages of employees working on an automobile assembly line, for example.)

DIRECT MATERIAL COSTS: Expenditures for specifically identifiable items with physical properties that become a part of a finished product. (The steel, headlights, tires, etc. in an automobile.)

DISCRETIONARY COST: A cost element over which management does have control. (An advertising budget is an example of a discretionary cost. We can spend it, but we don't have to if we change our minds.)

FASB: "FASBEE" – The Financial Accounting Standards Board is the entity that prescribes GAAP.

FINANCIAL ACCOUNTING: The branch of accounting that concerns itself with the preparation of financial statements for use by creditors and investors to assist those persons in making various decisions regarding the extension of credit or in becoming an owner, in whole or in part, of the entity whose financial statements they are evaluating.

FIXED COST: A cost element that DOES NOT vary, in total, with the volume of production. (Factory rent is a fixed cost.)

GAAP: "GAP" – Generally accepted accounting principles; a set of rules that provide guidance in the preparation of financial statements in an attempt to provide uniformity in the accounting treatment of various financial transactions.

GROSS PROFIT: The difference between sales price and cost of goods sold. Also known as margin or gross profit on sales.

GROSS PROFIT PERCENTAGE: Gross profit divided by sales. ($50 gross profit divided by $150 in sales equals a gross profit percentage of 33%.)

IMA: The Institute of Management Accountants. This is the professional society of persons who specialize in management accounting, and they offer the professional CMA for Certified Management Accountant. The Institute publishes the journal, Strategic Finance each month.

INDIRECT LABOR: Expenditures for wages of employees who are not directly and physically involved in the production process. (Factory maintenance workers, supervisory salaries. etc.)

INDIRECT MATERIAL: Expenditures for minor components of finished products that are difficult to trace to a specific item, or the expense of tracing the cost doesn't warrant the practice. (Screws used to install a glove box in an automobile.)

Indirect Labor and Indirect Material are part of Manufacturing Overhead.

LINE POSITION: An employee who is directly involved in the manufacture and sale of products or services to customers of the company.

MANUFACTURING COSTS: Consists of three elements: Direct Material Cost, Direct Labor Cost, and Manufacturing Overhead.

MANUFACTURING OVERHEAD: All costs of production that are not direct labor or direct material. (Electricity to run machinery.)

MARGIN OF SAFETY: A theoretical dollar amount that suggests to management an amount by which decreases in sales may be absorbed before the organization begins to experience general losses.

MARGINAL COST: The added cost of selecting one plan of action over another. (Travel by bus costs $50, while traveling by air costs $150. The marginal cost (also known as differential cost) is $100.

MASTER BUDGET: Management's plan of operations, with dollar values assigned to the various operating segments and functions.

MIXED COSTS: A cost element that is a combination of some fixed and some variable costs. (A water bill with a flat fee (the fixed part), and a per-gallon charge over a base amount of water consumed (the variable part.)

OPPORTUNITY COST: The financial consequences of choosing Plan A over Plan B. (Plan B is purchasing a bank certificate of deposit that pays 6 percent interest. Plan A is purchasing a new machine. The "opportunity cost" is the interest income foregone by not buying the certificate.)

PERIOD COST: An expense that does not become part of the cost of a product or service. The expense appears on the income statement in the period in which it is incurred. (A telephone bill is an example of a period cost.)

PRIME COST: The combination of direct material and direct labor costs.

PRODUCT MIX: When a company sells more than a single product or service its combination of offerings is called its product mix. If you are in the restaurant business and your menu includes pizzas, pasta dinners and Italian sausage/beef sandwiches, that group of offerings constitutes your "product mix."

PROFIT PLANNING: A synonym for budgeting, the process through which operational plans are assigned monetary values. The profit plan is used as a guidebook that leads to desired end-results and also serves as a control tool to measure progress along the way to the desired outcome resulting from management's efforts.

RELEVANT COST: Cost items that must be considered when making financial decisions, because they will be effected by, and will have an effect upon, the financial results of a decision that is made. (In making a decision between serving hamburgers or hot dogs for your next backyard cookout, the cost of the meat products is relevant; the cost of the paper plates from which they will be eaten is not relevant.)

RELEVANT RANGE: A range of production volumes within which the assumptions we make regarding cost behaviors are valid. When we stray outside of the relevant range we must reconsider, and perhaps adjust our cost behavior assumptions.

RISK-REWARD CURVE: A graphic presentation that depicts the relationship between assumptions of investment risks with the anticipated rewards (earnings) one might expect to receive for accepting a given level of risk.

STAFF POSITION: An employee whose responsibility is to provide the resources needed by line-position personnel to carry out their duties. (Manufacturing is line, and purchasing is staff.)

STANDARD COST: A value determined by consensus between engineers, accountants, purchasing managers, and manufacturing managers. This value is "what it should cost" to make a particular product. There may be standard costs for direct mail, direct labor, and manufacturing overhead, the sum of which is the standard cost for a product.

STEP-VARIABLE COST: A cost element whose cost of acquisition is not linear. This element may only be acquired in "bunches." (The addition of an employee is an example. Barring temporary help, we cannot acquire just one more hour of labor cost; we must acquire a full 40 hours per-week of added labor cost.)

STRATEGIC FINANCE: The monthly journal of the IMA.

SUNK COST: An expenditure that has already been made, and nothing that can be done will change that fact. (You purchase Machine X only to learn one month later that Machine Y is much better. The expenditure for Machine X is a sunk cost; you cannot change that.) Sunk costs are ignored when making decisions concerning the future, and all decisions affect the future, none change the past.

UNAVOIDABLE COST: In a decision-making situation, this is a cost that will remain unchanged in the future, regardless of which decision is made. Unavoidable costs are always irrelevant in decision-making situations.

VARIABLE COST: A cost element that does vary, in total, in connection with the volume of production. (The meat used to produce hamburgers is a variable cost.)

NOW THIS IS TRICKY! **Fixed** costs stay the same in total, but move up and down at the unit level, based upon volume. **Variable** cost stays the same at the unit level, but moves up and down in total, in connection with production volume.

(If an automobile battery has a cost of $40, it will stay at $40 per automobile regardless of how many automobiles are produced. But in total, the more automobiles we produce, the more total variable costs we will accumulate. On the other hand, if the factory manager is paid $6,000 per month (a fixed cost), the expenditure in total will remain the same no matter how many automobiles are produced, but the cost per unit will change. If we produce 6,000 automobiles, we will have a cost of $1 per unit. If we produce only 3,000 units, the cost will be $2 per unit.)

VARIABLE COSTING: A system of reporting wherein all fixed manufacturing overhead is charged as a period cost and does not enter into the computation of the unit cost of goods manufactured. This system IS NOT acceptable for external reporting purposes.

Donald R. Dignam, MBA, CPA

About the Author

The author's preparation for writing this book includes more than thirty-five years of professional experience in public accounting, private industry and the not-for profit sector. He has held positions as President of his own CPA firm, Chief Financial Officer, Treasurer and Chief Operating Officer of local, national and International corporations.

His articles have appeared in a variety of trade and professional journals, and he has appeared as a speaker at numerous continuing education programs, business forums and seminars, where his audiences have rated his presentations as excellent.

The author earned the degree Bachelor of Business Education from Chicago State University and was awarded the degree of Master of Business Administration from DePaul University. In addition, Mr. Dignam has earned Fellowships in the American College of Health Care Executives and the Healthcare Financial Management Association. He is a licensed CPA in the States of Illinois and Indiana.

Students at Indiana University South Bend consistently rate him as being superior to excellent as an instructor.

Printed in the United States
939500005B